SPECIAL EDUCATOR'S SURVIVAL GUIDE

Practical Techniques and Materials for Supervision and Instruction

David B. Barnes, Ed.D. and Cheryle K. Barnes, M.Ed.

THE CENTER FOR APPLIED RESEARCH IN EDUCATION
West Nyack, New York 10995

10   9   8   7   6   5   4   3   2   1

Printed in the United States of America

Library of Congress Cataloging-in-Publication Data

Barnes, David B.
    Special educator's survival guide: practical techniques and
materials for supervision and instruction / David B. Barnes and
Cheryle K. Barnes.
        p.   cm.
    Bibliography: p.
    Includes index.
    ISBN 0-87628-784-4
    1. Special education—Handbooks, manuals, etc. I. Barnes,
Cheryle K.   II. Title.
LC3965.B35   1989
371.9—dc19   89-567
                                                             CIP

ISBN 0-87628-784-4

**THE CENTER FOR APPLIED
RESEARCH IN EDUCATION**
BUSINESS & PROFESSIONAL DIVISION
A division of Simon & Schuster
West Nyack, New York 10995

This book is dedicated to our parents who taught us this philosophy; to our teachers, colleagues, and students who helped us operationalize our philosophy; and to our children who we hope will live by it.

About the Authors

DAVID B. BARNES (Ed.D., Rutgers University, New Jersey; M.Ed., University of Maine; B.S., Springfield College, Massachusetts), has been involved with education and psychology for over 30 years, and has held the positions of regular classroom teacher, Director of Guidance, university faculty member, and clinical psychologist. Since 1977, he has been involved with special education administration, first as a Supervisor of Special Services for two school boards in Nova Scotia, and most recently as School Psychologist and Special Education Administrator in Vermont. Dr. Barnes is the author of several articles on special education and has been a featured speaker at national conferences in both the United States and Canada.

CHERYLE K. BARNES (M.Ed., Acadia University, Wolfville, Nova Scotia; B.A., Miami University, Oxford, Ohio) has been involved with special education for over 20 years. During this time, she has been a regular classroom teacher, resource teacher, special education teacher, and diagnostician. She has also worked as Special Education Consultant for Mental Health and the Cape Breton Child Guidance Center in Nova Scotia. Mrs. Barnes has also been a speaker at national special education conferences in the United States and Canada.

About This Guide

The Special Educator's Survival Guide was written because of the need for a book that presents a consistent philosophy, principles of application, and concrete examples of successful special education programs. The book presents major issues that many special education teachers and administrators may find difficult to deal with in their own particular settings. For example:

- In Chapter 1, the development of the service delivery model is included along with the major considerations that must be addressed, with an example of the application of these considerations in an actual model for service delivery in a school system. This chapter deals with a continuum of special programs needed for the wide variety of student needs encountered in any school system. Included are the development of pre-referral procedures, referral procedures, and conducting the case conference.

- Chapter 2 considers the preventative approach in special education, discussing not only the prevention of needless labeling and programs in the school situation but also linking up the school delivery system with a preventative program in the community. Programs based on the early identification of high-risk infants and follow-up programs based on home intervention are offered. In addition, this chapter deals with the need for programs of parent education and the variety of formats that can be utilized for delivering this service to parents.

- Chapter 3 details the "why" and "how" of preschool screening. This chapter deals with important topics such as preparing parents for preschool screening programs and gives samples of both commercial and school-based screening programs and their proper utilization for the benefit of students. Included in this chapter are several handouts for parents.

- Chapter 4 reflects the authors' philosophy concerning assessment and includes such topics as factors for consideration, and functional areas in student assessment, sources of assessment data, and the relationship of physical factors to the overall assessment procedure. It also deals with the use and misuse of standardized testing and contains a variety of reproducible forms including: precision referral forms; educational assessment profiles and their use in explaining results to both classroom teachers and parents; and guidelines for parents when meeting with teachers, pediatricians, and psychologists. This chapter discusses the critical approach to and sequence involved in student placement.

• Chapter 5 reviews the role of the resource teacher and divides this role into the major components of assessment, programming, instruction, consultation, and training volunteers. Included in this chapter are the principles of individualized programming based on the educational assessment. It contains several sample programs designed to assist the "total child." These programs are specifically designed for use at home, in the regular classroom, and in a tutorial setting. There are helpful forms to assist resource teachers in using their own observations to determine children's learning needs and which adaptive procedures to use for individual children and their unique learning styles. Also included are sample integrated lesson plans that can help the resource teacher assist children in their major areas of need through a variety of in-school settings. There are sections in Chapter 5 dealing with using community resources in programming for individual children and also guidelines and suggestions for including volunteer programs within the school setting. The role of the resource teacher when dealing with older elementary school and secondary school students is considered, as well as a major emphasis on how this role differs from that of a resource teacher dealing with very young students in an elementary school.

• Chapter 6 describes the process of building special class curriculums based on goals and objectives for both full-time and part-time special class placements. This chapter gives concrete suggestions on involving parents in curriculum planning and contains goals and objectives by age group for students with differing degrees of need. It contains sample curriculum guides for any students based on the goals and objectives previously outlined.

• Chapter 7 is concerned with the many aspects of evaluation including that of staff, programs, individual students, and the entire delivery system. Included are several reproducible forms for parents and teachers to evaluate programs for individual children; and sample reports to send home to parents for children receiving services within special classes or under the direction of a resource teacher and regular classroom teachers.

At the conclusion of each chapter is a list of the references discussed in the chapter. Since many of these references include materials, the name and address of each publisher are also given.

We sincerely hope that you will find the practical applications, program descriptions, and reproducible forms convenient and useable. However, our greatest desire is that the philosophy and principles upon which the practical aspects of *The Special Educator's Survival Guide* are based will not be overshadowed.

David B. Barnes
Cheryle K. Barnes

Contents

List of Figures

Acknowledgments

The authors wish to express deep appreciation to the many individuals who have been an inspiration, and to our many teachers, colleagues, and students who have helped to formulate the philosophy and principles described in this book.

The authors would like to thank both the Cape Breton County Municipal School Board and the Lunenburg County District School Board for their continued support in accepting the model proposed and by giving moral and financial support to the implementation of the programs described in the book.

A very special thanks to the principals and teachers who have accepted the model and through hard work have made it work to the benefit of the children in their charge.

Special thanks to Evelyn Fazio, Editor, for her encouragement and guidance in revising this book; and to Nancy Joudrey for her typing of the manuscript.

Also, a special thanks to Matthew and Bryan for sacrificing their time with Mom and Dad so that this book could be completed.

Development of the Service Delivery Model

Education is a social process . . .
Education is growth . . .
Education is not preparation for life;
Education is life itself.

John Dewey

The above quote from John Dewey should be kept in mind when critical decisions are made about the development of a delivery system for Special Education. This quote appears to be well founded in that many researchers have concluded that the value of many social interactions is not the product but the process involved in the planning and decision making. With current trends toward "back to basics" and maintaining standards, process may be overlooked in deference to performance. When this becomes the case, many students feel alone and alienated and suffer from lack of self-esteem and self-confidence. This certainly is not the way to prepare students for a rewarding and enriched life in society. As educators, we must continually search to find a variety of ways to improve the self-esteem of all students but especially those having "special needs" within our school systems.

THE IMPORTANCE OF SELF-ESTEEM

Mrs. Gloria Blum, author and educational consultant, who has developed several programs to allow teachers and students to practice helping each other feel good about themselves, describes self-esteem as: ". . . not exclusively the process of feeling unique and special. Self-esteem includes a balance with a sense of belonging, a sense of inclusion that is rooted within a deeper knowing that each of us are also like other people." The primary feeling that a class or group should give to each individual is, "WE ARE NOT COMPLETE WITHOUT YOU." These feelings and concepts of self-esteem become even more important as children move into adolescence and are the starting points for sex education programs among adolescents. According to noted sex researcher and educator, Dr. Sol Gordon, director of the Institute for Family Research and Education at Syracuse University, "Young people who feel good about themselves are not available for exploitation and do not exploit others."

There is considerable concern today about child and adolescent suicide. The link between suicide and depression has been made for a long time; however, often unwittingly we ignore the link between depression and loss of self-esteem. All major theories today expound the fact that loss of self-esteem is the central feature of depression. Students in our schools with special needs are certainly the high risk group for loss of self-esteem which may lead to depression and the possibility of suicide.

One of the basic principles then in establishing and constructing a system for the delivery of Special Education Services is that self-esteem of students must be a priority.

CONSIDERATIONS IN SYSTEM DEVELOPMENT

The authors, in discussing the other considerations in system development, would suggest that like self-esteem, other philosophical issues be dealt with prior to the establishment of policies, remembering that there is nothing quite as practical as a workable philosophy. The reason for this is that it makes future decision making much easier, whether it be community decisions regarding school board policy or individual decisions regarding children within the system. Following philosophical issues, the individuals concerned must deal with the needs and the strengths of the area and develop a model for the most comprehensive delivery of services to both "special needs" children and their parents. There is nothing more confusing to parents, teachers, and others, than to have many of their questions answered with seemingly unrelated policy statements and to have these statements treated as though they came down off the mountain in Moses' other hand. This leads to several considerations that must be dealt with in system development.

- First of all, the system must be simple and easy to understand by all individuals directly involved including: special education teachers, regular classroom teachers, school administrators, parents, and school board members.

- The system must also offer practical and concrete suggestions to all the individuals involved and must be capable of being utilized as a tool for the delivery of services as well as planning.

- The system, when developed, must be an integral and leading part of the community and not a separate entity unique to itself. The system must attempt to coordinate and utilize not only educational facilities, but those facilities in the community such as home, church, and other agencies.

- The system should reflect modern thought in education and must, in some way, deal with "mainstreaming," parents' rights, early identification of learning problems, and the "total child."

- The system must offer a continuum of services which provides a variety of methods and the right amount of "special help" so that each student requiring assistance receives it in the most appropriate way.

SPECIAL CONSIDERATIONS IN RURAL AREAS

Two words which we frequently use in our vocabulary are "rural" and "urban." They mean very different things to many people and have tended to be described in a variety of ways. Their meanings can be as diverse as: distance from a metropolitan center, population, access to services, primary occupational groups, and population density.

School systems have only, in fairly recent history, become concerned with access to services. Prior to this movement, children who could not fit into the traditional school system in any area were excluded, and it was parental responsibility to find alternative educational programs appropriate for their children's needs. This has not changed and many of the services that school systems wish to access are not those directly offered by the schools themselves but those dealing with health services and social services of a specialized nature. It is these specialized medical and social services, not educational services, that tend to be centered in urban areas, making it more difficult for rural school systems to take advantage of these services.

An additional complicating factor in the field of Special Education is that most of the Special Education programs that are in existence today also had their roots in urban areas where Special Education programs were developed before those in rural areas. In the initial stages of the development of urban Special Education programs, many school districts insisted upon having specialists from medical fields involved in the establishment of the programs, as well as in selection committees, and as advisors and consultants to the teachers and others who worked in these programs. When the movement for "the right to an education for all children" moved into rural areas, rural school systems turned to their urban friends for a model to establish programs and policies. It soon became evident that this urban model could not be transferred directly because rural areas did not have the pediatric neurologists, child psychiatrists, educational audiologists, and a raft of other specialized professionals to rely on for the development and maintenance of their Special Education programs. It also became evident that when specialists were available, they were used more as consultants rather than delivering direct service to children. The specialist role in rural systems became one of assessment of children and developing programs to be delivered by parents, teachers, aides, and volunteers.

A further distinction between the delivery of services in an urban system and a rural system is the "ownership of the program." Urban areas tend to have a larger central office staff and often take a majority of the responsibility for supervision of classes and programs within individual schools. In rural areas, the principal of the school must accept ownership of and responsibility for the program and rely more upon central office staff as consultants to assist themselves and teachers in making their programs operate as effectively as possible.

Due to the specialized nature of many classes which were established in urban areas, it has been difficult to move students out of these classes. This is often because of fear on the part of regular classroom teachers. As a result many urban areas have not moved as rapidly to place as many children as possible in the least restrictive environment. Often teachers in rural areas have had a great deal more experience working with "special" children because there were no alternatives. In addition to this, many of them have had more experience in multilevel classrooms and in providing the specialized services such as art, music, and physical education, than have their urban counterparts.

Many of the foregoing statements and examples are generalizations. However, it is felt that Special Education programs must develop their own model based on an assessment of the strengths in each community, and must find methods to mobilize these strengths in order to develop the best possible program. It is indeed easy to look at what the small community lacks and use this as a basis for not delivering as many services as possible for "special" children and their parents. One must remember the motto of the Christophers: "It is better to light one candle than to curse the darkness." Earlier, it was pointed out that many rural areas center upon their weakness, which is primarily "lack of specialized services," both within the educational system and in the areas of health and social service facilities. Some important strengths that can be found in rural areas are:

- a more stable population base;
- a greater sense of community;
- more person-to-person communication among both professionals and parents.

A variety of ways that these strengths can be utilized in system development will be dealt with in the following chapters.

CHANGING THE SYSTEM

The development of a new model of Special Education delivery is extremely difficult in areas where there are established systems, especially one that is based on a great many special classes for children with a variety of diagnostic labels. In addition to this, the passage of public law 94-142 in the United States has led to the lumping of children with like diagnostic labels into special schools and special classes often without enough consideration to their unique learning styles and strengths as individuals. The maintenance of this system in many states is rationalized by many individuals who feel that if it is not followed, money will not be available. This has proven to be false in Massachusetts, where it is now illegal to label a child. One may describe a child's learning and behavior and still offer adequate services.

The lack of integration between regular education and special education has also increased the labeling process to the point of making educators believe that this is the only way in which children can receive the special kind of assistance that they need. Dr. Laurence Lieberman, in his book *Preventing Special Education . . . for Those Who Don't Need It*, states that current educational research and literature is replete with reference to overkill in every facet of Special Education service delivery: referrals, testing, programming, conferencing, paperwork, diagnosing, labeling, and above all, promoting Special Education as the means by which regular education problems are solved. It is also interesting to note that many experts associated with education believe that the vast majority of children having school-based problems do not have anything inherently wrong with them.

THE TEACHER IS THE KEY

The authors firmly believe that both principals and teachers must first and foremost have a mission of service to all of their students. In addition, they must have the ability to conceptualize the present functioning of their students and to assist them in establishing realistic future goals. Teachers must learn to evaluate themselves in terms of reducing the gap between their goals and their actual teaching practices. Figure 1-1 has proven helpful in assisting teachers to assess their own functioning and also to plan for improving their performance in the future. This form can be used periodically by teachers to avoid getting into a "rut." The form has also been used by teachers to discuss their own performance and to share ideas with "valued colleagues" and supervisors.

Teachers whose classroom practices are in line with their goals and philosophy usually achieve much greater job satisfaction than teachers with wide discrepancies between their goals and practices. Job satisfaction is an important aspect in preventing teacher "burnout" and in increasing the self-esteem of teachers. It is difficult for a teacher with poor self-esteem to effectively assist students toward increased self-esteem.

IS LABELING CHILDREN NECESSARY?

As special educators, we must begin to recognize that we are not a system unto ourselves, any more than a school is a system that exists outside a

TEACHER SELF-ASSESSMENT

DO I:	USUALLY	SOMETIMES	NEVER
• Devote time to planning?			
• Plan for more than one activity to happen at a time?			
• Plan for group flexibility?			
• Think in terms of students' needs rather than grade-level expectations?			
• Plan for activities designed to promote a positive classroom environment?			
• Reward students?			
• Have a list of student learning objectives adapted for my classroom?			
• Continually assess students using multiple approaches?			
• Have appropriate assessment for each learning objective?			
• Provide alternatives to the textbook?			
• Have an array of learning activities pertaining to acquiring each learning objective?			
• Design these activities to include multilevel, multimedia, and multiarea activities?			
• Have activities that incorporate optional learning modes: large group, small groups, paired situations, one-to-one instruction, and independent study?			
• Match learning activities to the student's learnign style, interests, achievement, and peer relationships?			

DO I:	USUALLY	SOMETIMES	NEVER
• Use interest centers, learning centers, and learning stations?			
• Have only the furniture I need in the classroom?			
• Utilize all available space?			
• Accept student decisions?			
• Encourage independence?			
• Try alternatives?			
• Analyze my teaching style and develop a plan for self-improvement?			
• Discuss problems with my peers and value the opinions of others?			
• Have the support of the administration?			
• Train students in decision making?			
• Share teaching responsibility with students?			
• Share learning responsibility with students?			
• Include the student in parent conferences?			
• Make the student aware of the objectives for his/her learning activities?			
• Encourage students to select their own learning objectives?			
• Involve each student in self-assessment and analysis of assessments?			
• Provide the opportunity for students to participate in the selection of activities to achieve an objective?			

DO I:	USUALLY	SOMETIMES	NEVER
• Communicate expectations to students (outcomes, checkpoints, sequence of activities)?			
• Help each student achieve some success?			
• Permit the student to function at a comfortable pace?			
• Train the students to use equipment and materials and then trust the students to use them independently?			
• Train the students in the use of learning centers and stations?			
• Involve parents as volunteers?			
• Encourage parents to visit the classroom?			
• Keep parents informed about the learning program?			
• Use community resources?			

FIGURE 1-1

community. We are all part of a much bigger holistic design to help children to develop to their fullest potential in all ways possible.

The authors therefore suggest that all traditional labels be dropped in establishing the service delivery system for a school district. Although this may not be practical in some places because funding is based on using these labels, it is certainly a goal for which to aim. Some states have already passed legislation making it illegal to use these labels with regard to children. The cascade model of service delivery certainly is a helpful tool in viewing the levels of services required by students at any particular time and will be more fully explained later in this chapter. These levels must, however, be used on an individualized basis with students and must not become a replacement for traditional categories such as multihandicapped, TMH, EMH, LD, etc. The authors suggest that in rural areas, they have had considerable success in working with the system that categorizes children as highest need, high need, and other needy children. These are labels descriptive of the child's level of independent functioning at any given time. It is easily understood by professionals and laypersons as well and is descriptive of the level of service required for students rather than based on more traditional diagnostic labels. This system also allows for more flexibility in planning and movement of children as their level of independent functioning improves. This concept is certainly not new. As far back as 1971, James Mooney, director of diagnostic services for the Northern Suburban Special Education District in Illinois, presented a paper entitled "Softening of the Categories," in which he stated "Traditions, even when made of clay, tend to become hardened over time." Mooney further states that efforts to soften the categories lead to improved models for Special Education programming. The avoidance of medical-psychological labels in educational practice help educators focus more on each child's individual needs rather than on common needs of a group of children having a similar defect or problem. It is further suggested that terms such as brain damaged, schizophrenic, and even mentally defective have little to offer in a school frame of reference. A softening here, away from clinical labels, would constitute an important beginning as would a removal of classroom defectology titles. Why not just Special Education classes? In his paper, Mooney goes on to suggest several other important aspects; however, the bottom line in many areas is that funding is related to labeling. Educators must work to have this changed.

MAINSTREAMING

In the development of a model, certainly mainstreaming must be dealt with as a major philosophical issue. (See Figure 1-2.) The term "mainstreaming" is not only a philosophical issue, but in many communities has become an emotional issue. This has polarized many groups and school systems and has prevented the development of the types of services that people would like to see for children having "special needs."

WHAT IS "MAINSTREAMING"?

The term "mainstreaming" has been used frequently and in different ways during the last few years. Along with its varied meanings has come confusion regarding what the word really means. While there may not be a definition that is universally agreed on, there are some basic themes that can be looked to for an understanding of the intent of mainstreaming.

MAINSTREAMING IS:

● Providing the most appropriate education for each child in the least restrictive setting.

● Looking at the educational needs of children instead of clinical or diagnostic labels such as mentally handicapped, learning disabled, physically handicapped, hearing impaired, or gifted.

● Looking for and creating alternatives that will help general educators serve children with learning or adjustment problems in the regular setting. Some approaches being used to help achieve this are consulting teachers, methods and materials specialists, itinerant teachers, and resource room teachers.

● Uniting the skills of general education and special education so that all children may have equal educational opportunity.

MAINSTREAMING IS NOT:

● Wholesale return of all exceptional children in special classes to regular classes.

● Permitting children with special needs to remain in regular classrooms without the support services that they need.

● Ignoring the need of some children for a more specialized program than can be provided in the general education program.

● Less costly than serving children in special self-contained classrooms.

This material is provided as a service from the Council for Exceptional Children.

FIGURE 1-2

REASONS FOR MAINSTREAMING

Utilizing this concept of mainstreaming, there are several significant reasons for school boards to move toward increasingly more mainstreaming. First, it is a model of democracy which is created by establishing an educational environment where the worth and dignity of each student is acknowledged, and where individual differences are recognized and accepted. Also, it is a means for educating disabled children in an environment that more closely resembles the real world. Regular program students receive experience with students they are not likely to meet in a society where the disabled are segregated. Segregated programs and institutions have had minimal success. Labeling and segregating exceptional children increases their distinct categorization and stigmatization.

THE SCHOOL'S ROLE IN PREVENTION

In addition to the foregoing considerations and philosophical issues, the Special Education model of services must consider and deal with the school's role in prevention, which is effective liaison with:

- preschool programs;
- medical personnel;
- social service personnel;
- community agencies interested in the welfare of children and their families.

In addition to this, they must deal with some form of preschool evaluation and screening designed, not to label children, but to understand and assist them in their development. Although in many places, programs for preschool handicapped are available, there are many rural areas where this is not true. It is suggested that educators, as the largest professional group in any community, become involved in establishing a variety of preschool programs to prevent the need for additional Special Education services when children enter the school system. This may be accomplished by school boards offering professional support to these programs, or by local teacher unions or associations giving financial and professional support.

PRE-REFERRAL AND REFERRAL PROCEDURES

Each school board, in developing a system of service delivery, must deal with both pre-referral and referral procedures. There have been many suggestions in dealing with pre-referral procedures such as teacher assistance teams, and in-school Special Education committees to assist teachers who have children with learning problems in the classroom, and to eliminate unnecessary referrals for complete and formal assessment. Once this has been dealt with, a procedure for referrals can be established.

PARENT INVOLVEMENT

In education, parents as well as students are consumers and must be treated with respect and dignity. Parents must be involved with Special Education programs from the moment of referral on. Having lived with their own children for several years, they certainly can give valuable information regarding the child, his/her strengths and weaknesses, and his/her development over the years. They must be involved in the program planning and decision making concerning appropriate placement (legislated by public law 94-142 in the United States but a healthy practice in other parts of the world). Parents should also be involved in programming and evaluation as well as in establishing goals and objectives for their children.

INITIAL CASE CONFERENCE

The initial case conference following assessment should include the parents, the school principal or other pertinent administrator, the classroom teacher, the Special Education teacher, and the individual responsible for assessment. During this case conference, a program should be planned for each student containing:

- a home program;
- a classroom teacher program;
- if necessary, a tutorial program;
- community programs to assist the child in his development.

COMMUNITY PROGRAMS

The aspects for consideration up to this point do not differ from urban to rural areas; however, when considering community programs mentioned previously, school personnel may have to take a leadership role within the community to develop necessary programs to assist children having special needs. The authors suggest the following:

- a primary prevention program in cooperation with local hospitals and/ or public health department;
- specialized and regular summer camps;
- adapted recreation programs;
- comprehensive volunteer programs;
- more adequate and in-depth professional development programs for both Special Education and regular classroom teachers;
- development of parental support groups and parent support programs;
- provision of needed consultation and expertise to preschool programs and nursery schools;

- a comprehensive program of public relations so that the general public and local professionals are aware of what you are attempting to accomplish.

THE IMPORTANCE OF TEAMWORK

In establishing a service delivery model for any school district, teamwork is of the utmost importance. No one person or group has all the skills or energy to put meaningful programs into operation. The school board and senior administration of the school system must be fully informed and supportive of all areas of the program. School principals who are responsible for daily supervision and much implementation must feel that their concerns are being addressed and that their thoughts and feelings are considered in the overall planning. Parents of students must have adequate opportunities to have changes in the system explained to them, to ask questions, and to make suggestions and comments. Staff feelings, of both special educators and regular class teachers, must be solicited and dealt with as appropriately as possible. In addition to staff feelings, the evaluation and placement of staff in most appropriate positions is certainly a high priority consideration in the development of any system. It often seems like a paradox when administrators talk about individualization of instruction for children and yet expect all staff to function equally. Administrators have the responsibility to recognize individual strengths and weaknesses of staff and place them in the most appropriate positions. When requiring change of staff positions, they must be given adequate support and training so that they might make the greatest contribution to the program.

Teachers often become extremely frustrated when they have good ideas and are not given support or freedom to implement them. Many valuable programs and some of the best ideas result from the interest and skills of individual staff members who are given necessary support and encouragement in trying out their new ideas. It may truly be said that "teacher burnout" is not the result of overwork but of feelings of frustration and impotence. The final team member that must be dealt with is the Special Education administrator, whose role and responsibility is to plan, discuss, and revise the basic system of service delivery for the school district. The following is an example of a model developed by the authors for the delivery of Special Education Services. The authors caution the reader that this is not a "what" or "how to" model but is simply an example of how the foregoing considerations in system development were dealt with in one school district.

A MODEL FOR THE DELIVERY
OF SPECIAL EDUCATION SERVICES

This model delineates the way in which a continuum of Special Education Services is delivered in a rural school system. The philosophy underlying this model is mainstreaming.

Mainstreaming as a term should not be misconstrued. In addition to this there is no particular service that will meet all of the needs of all of the children in Special Education. Therefore, what has been developed is a continuum of services ranging from supplying children in regular classes with special equipment and/or materials to arranging for instruction in a residential setting, as well as a variety of services between these two extremes. The important thing is that a child is placed in the least restrictive environment (most productive environment), following the best assessment possible and is returned as rapidly as possible toward regular classes and regular curriculum. A model outlining the various parts of this and the explanation of each is included with this document (Figure 1-3).

In addition, a Special Education Service cannot operate in isolation and must have the regular classroom teacher as the key person in the delivery of services. This teacher, however, must not be allowed to stand alone but must receive the necessary support from Special Education personnel as well as others in the community.

In order to work effectively, the Special Education Model of Services should be linked with a Prevention Model (also included with this document, Figure 1-4) which includes items such as preschool screening, involvement with preschool programs in the community, and liaison with medical personnel, social service personnel, and other community agencies interested in the welfare of children and their families.

RESOURCE TEACHERS

The majority of students having special needs can be adequately serviced by regular classroom teachers and resource teachers working together. All schools, regardless of size, must have the services of a resource teacher. The role of resource teacher is discussed in Chapter 5.

SPECIAL CLASSES

It is suggested that the special classes be divided in two ways, highest-need classes and high-need classes. This system of division, rather than an arbitrary diagnostic categorization such as EMH, TMH, autistic, emotionally disturbed, learning disability, and so forth, has several advantages: it talks more in terms of a child's functional level regardless of the diagnostic label, and is made on the basis of multiple assessments, only one of which is intellectual level, which often is not nearly as important as the ability to function independently or adaptive behavior. A further advantage of this classification is that it allows some leeway in planning for individual children and in placing them in the most appropriate educational environment. Special classes may not be possible in all schools; however, they should be strategically placed in selected schools throughout the school district.

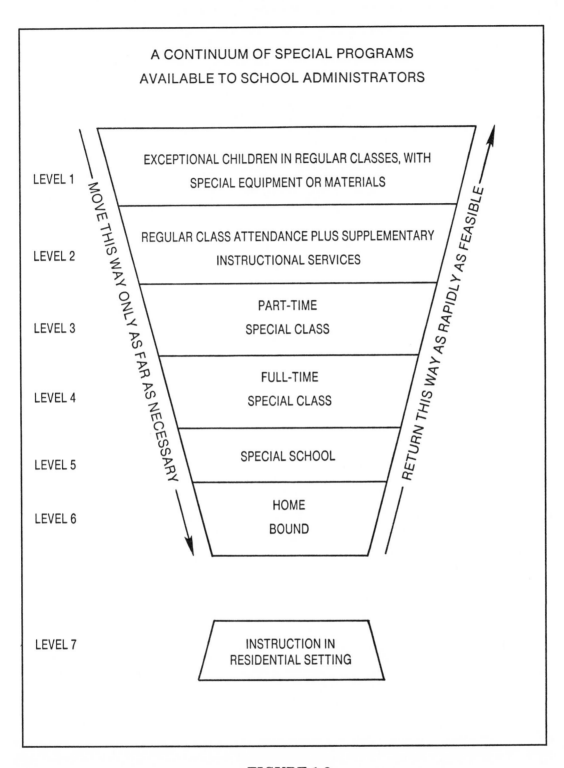

A CONTINUUM OF SPECIAL PROGRAMS
AVAILABLE TO SCHOOL ADMINISTRATORS

LEVEL 1 — EXCEPTIONAL CHILDREN IN REGULAR CLASSES, WITH SPECIAL EQUIPMENT OR MATERIALS

LEVEL 2 — REGULAR CLASS ATTENDANCE PLUS SUPPLEMENTARY INSTRUCTIONAL SERVICES

LEVEL 3 — PART-TIME SPECIAL CLASS

LEVEL 4 — FULL-TIME SPECIAL CLASS

LEVEL 5 — SPECIAL SCHOOL

LEVEL 6 — HOME BOUND

LEVEL 7 — INSTRUCTION IN RESIDENTIAL SETTING

MOVE THIS WAY ONLY AS FAR AS NECESSARY

RETURN THIS WAY AS RAPIDLY AS FEASIBLE

FIGURE 1-3

15

Placement of a student in a special class should not mean that he/she is not integrated with regular class students for such activities as:

- homeroom;
- physical education;
- music;
- art;
- field trips;
- special activities, e.g. Christmas concerts;
- academic subjects where possible.

PRINCIPLES OF OPERATION

- Get rid of traditional labels.
- New means of classifying children:
  (1) highest need;
  (2) high need;
  (3) other needy children.
- New criteria for placement in Special Education Program:
  (1) intellectual ability;
  (2) adaptive behavior.
- All children in Special Education should be on an individual program based on diagnostic assessment.
- Increased parental involvement in program:
  (1) in assessment;
  (2) in decision making;
  (3) in evaluation and programming;
  (4) in volunteer work;
  (5) parent support groups.
- Program evaluation:
  (1) done by classroom teachers;
  (2) parents' evaluation;
  (3) objective data evaluation.
- A Primary Prevention Model to eliminate as much unnecessary Special Education as possible.
- Working with community agencies.
- Comprehensive volunteer program.
- In-service programs.
- A comprehensive program of public relations.
- Evaluation and proper placement of existing staff:
  (1) staff training in the areas of assessment;

(2) continuity of program;
(3) evaluation of program.

PRE-REFERRAL PROCEDURE

Each school must establish a Special Education Committee with regular teaching staff, the principal or his delegate, and one Special Education staff person. The larger elementary schools may wish to have two Committees: one to deal with grades K(P) through 3; and the other to deal with grades 4 through 6. All teachers needing assistance in dealing with a specific child make an internal school referral to this Committee. The Committee discusses the child with his teacher and receives required information from previous teachers and makes suggestions to the classroom teacher for assisting this child. After a trial of one month, an evaluation is made as to the current status of the child and whether the suggestions developed by the Committee have been tried and how well they are working. If they are working, the Committee continues to assist the classroom teacher; however, if, after this time period, there still seems to be a great deal of difficulty, a formal referral procedure is put into operation.

REFERRAL PROCEDURE

Referral should be initiated by the teacher, who discusses the child with the principal. The principal forwards under his or her signature the referral sheet completed by the teacher to the Special Education Administrator, who assigns an assessment person(s) to complete the assessment needed to have a case conference regarding the student. Referrals should also be accepted from parents and other community professionals.

CASE CONFERENCE PROCEDURE

This should include the principal, the classroom teacher, the resource/reading teacher, the parents, and the individual who completed all or part of the assesssment. During the case conference the results of assessment and testing should be fully explained to all present; the options for possible placement to assist the child in his educational program should be explained to all individuals; the person conducting the case conference should give the professional recommendations; and the parents should be the ones responsible for making the decision as to which option or options might be followed. This is important, even if the professionals involved disagree with the parents' choice; it should be tried. If the parents make a "poor" choice, it can be reevaluated and changed. If, however, they are forced to accept a placement they do not agree with, they may always feel they had no input and that their choice was the correct one.

Following the case conference, a program should be planned for each student which will include as its parts:

- a home program;
- a classroom teacher program;
- a tutorial program (remediation may be done by a resource teacher or volunteer);
- a community program where necessary and/or available.

If, as a result of the case conference, it is determined that the most appropriate placement for a student would be a transfer to another school within the system that has a more appropriate program and facilities for assisting this particular child, then it is important that his home school and principal remain involved with the child and his parents. Copies of all reports must be sent from the receiving school to the sending school principal so that he or she is kept abreast of progress. The sending school principal should be involved and made aware of all parent/teacher conferences involving this child and should participate where possible.

ESTABLISHMENT OF REALISTIC GOALS

Each type of Special Education class in the system should have some basic goals and, when these are accomplished, the child should be moved toward the most "normal" placement; for example, elementary classes should work primarily on academic skills and independent behaviors with a hope toward assisting the child back into the regular classroom program. However, secondary school Special Education classes should have more realistic goals; for example, a secondary high-need class should emphasize employment, the possibility of specialized training, wise use of leisure time, and the application or practical use of learned academic skills rather than a continuation of learning academic skills for their own sake.

A CONTINUUM OF SPECIAL PROGRAMS

A child should follow a regular program in a regular class unless he obviously cannot cope with this situation. If the attempt to meet his needs with a regular program is found to be inappropriate, the options open to the school lie along a continuum ranging from using special equipment or materials in the regular class to instruction in a residential setting.

Level 1

Some exceptional children can receive appropriate instruction in regular classes using special equipment or materials. Special equipment might include a wheelchair for the physically handicapped child, a phonic ear for the hearing handicapped child and carrels for the highly distractible child. Special curriculum materials could be used to meet those instructional needs which are not being met by the regular curriculum.

Level 2

For children with the milder handicaps, it is preferable to enroll them in the regular class and meet their specific instructional needs on an individual tutoring basis or in small group instruction.

Levels 3 and 4

Special class placement, either part- or full-time, is indicated when the child's educational needs cannot be met by either of the options outlined in Levels 1 and 2. Most mentally handicapped children can have their needs met by part-time enrollment in special classes and in a regular program at their own level of achievement. Some might require full-time special class placement.

Because of the severity of the handicapping condition, some mentally handicapped children will require full-time special class placement for their academic program.

Level 5

Some school boards provide special schools for children with a variety of handicaps — emotionally disturbed, crippled, trainable mentally handicapped and multihandicapped. However, if at all possible, special classes should be maintained within a regular school rather than in a separate building. Being with normal children can help the handicapped child develop needed life skills.

Level 6

Because of physical/health handicaps, it may be necessary for some children to remain home for long periods. To avoid educational retardation, teachers may be provided to tutor such children in their homes. Homebound instruction should be carried out only where it is impossible for the child to be in school, and the child should return to school as soon as he is able to do so.

Level 7

The situation sometimes arises where, for the good of the child or the home, a residential setting is indicated. The 24-hour-a-day attention of a residential setting may be needed for the individual to acquire certain life skills or to modify certain behaviors.

In general, the further the child is removed from a "normal" school setting, the less desirable the program. The school should move the child away from regular class placement only as far as necessary, and move him back toward the regular class as rapidly as possible.

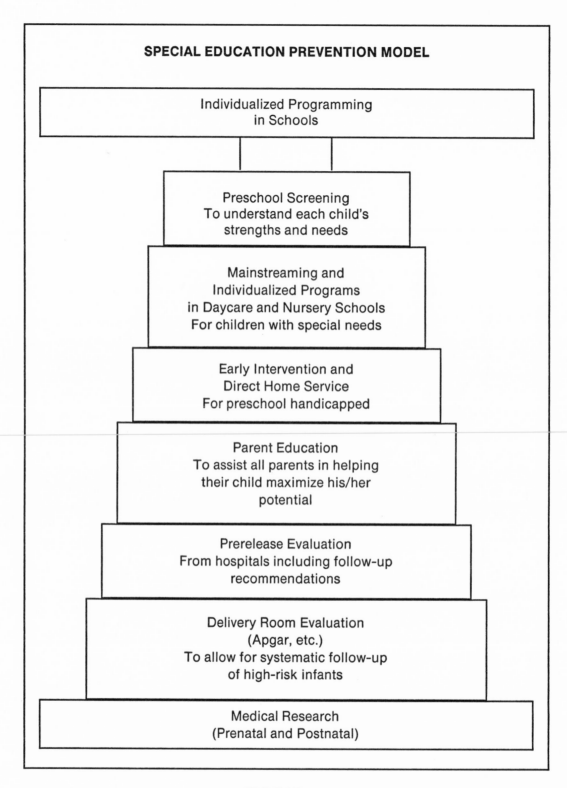

SPECIAL EDUCATION PREVENTION MODEL

Individualized Programming
in Schools

Preschool Screening
To understand each child's
strengths and needs

Mainstreaming and
Individualized Programs
in Daycare and Nursery Schools
For children with special needs

Early Intervention and
Direct Home Service
For preschool handicapped

Parent Education
To assist all parents in helping
their child maximize his/her
potential

Prerelease Evaluation
From hospitals including follow-up
recommendations

Delivery Room Evaluation
(Apgar, etc.)
To allow for systematic follow-up
of high-risk infants

Medical Research
(Prenatal and Postnatal)

FIGURE 1-4

In conclusion, the authors believe that any model of delivering special education services must be designed to protect the dignity of the children it serves and their parents. Without dignity and a healthy self-concept, no individual can reach his/her full potential. This may best be expressed by quoting the New Year's Message published by Simpsons following the United Nations Declaration of 1981 as the International Year of Disabled Persons.

He ran a country, he could not walk.
She wrote because a teacher's fingers helped her understand,
when she could neither see nor hear.
And they were called disabled.
You'll find the disabled among the presidents and clerks.
The typists and computer technicians.
Musicians, artists, teachers and ministers.
Philosophers and sportsmen.
They take their place in the world of business,
science and the arts.
They are handicapped only when society fails
to accommodate them.
Their participation is limited only to the level of equality
we will grant them.
So the fundamental questions are not, "What do they do?",
or even, "How do they do it?"
but rather, "What would we do without them? . . ."

CHAPTER 1 REFERENCE MATERIALS

Blum, Gloria, and Blum, Barry, *Feeling Good About Yourself*, Feeling Good Associates, Mill Valley, CA, 1981.

Address: Feeling Good Associates
             507 Palma Way
             Mill Valley, CA 94941

Council for Exceptional Children, "What Is Mainstreaming?" C.E.C., Reston, VA.

Address: Council for Exceptional Children
             1920 Association Drive
             Reston, VA 22091

Gordon, Sol, and Everly, Kathleen, "Increasing Self-Esteem in Vulnerable Students," Impact '85, Vol. 9, pages 1-4, Ed-U Press, Fayetteville, NY, 1985.

Address: Ed-U Press
             P.O. Box 583
             Fayetteville, NY 13066

Lieberman, Laurence M., *Preventing Special Education: For Those Who Don't Need It*, GloWorm Publications, Newton, MA, 1984.

Address: Nob Hill Press, Inc.
              Weston, MA 02193

Mooney, James A., "Softening the Categories," Unpublished.

Address: Stratford Center
              North Suburban Special Education District
              760 Red Oak Lane
              Highland Park, IL 60035

The Preventative Approach in Special Education

If you have built castles in the air,
your work need not be lost;
that is where they should be.
Now put foundations under them.

Henry David Thoreau

The preventative approach in Special Education is difficult to describe as is prevention in many fields of human service endeavors. It is, however, a viable philosophical approach which can operate effectively through appropriate community organizations and coordinated efforts between professionals in the fields of health, education, and social services. Prevention in Special Education is an essential part of the mainstreaming model, in that it is the development of services designed to assist children so that they may cope in public schools in the least restrictive environment possible.

All programs which are designed to identify children having developmental difficulties and to help parents and early childhood workers to assist these children prior to their entrance in school, must be considered a preventative aspect of Special Education.

The conditions responsible for the developmental delays cannot be prevented. However, what can be prevented through early identification and programming is the degree of the delays and also the amount of "special" services required by children when they enter school.

In many fields, the concept of prevention has gradually moved to identifying individuals at risk at much earlier ages than once was thought to be feasible or possible. Perhaps the most difficult part of developing a preventative program is that in a bureaucracy, no one seems to be responsible. Therefore, many agencies and professionals in the community must become involved in establishing a variety of preventative programs designed for early identification of children having difficulties and for assistance to these children and their parents.

This acceptance of responsibility and working together among agencies may be easier to accomplish in rural areas than it is in urban areas. This is perhaps due to the fact that there is usually increased personal contact in communication among professionals involved.

INFANT IDENTIFICATION AND FOLLOW-UP

Advances in medical science, especially in the field of neonatalogy, is making it possible for many infants with a variety of difficulties to survive. These are infants that a few years ago would have either died at delivery or succumbed from complications shortly after. This fact, coupled with improved screening of newborns, certainly indicates that many of these children should be considered at risk and their development monitored. Dr. Pamela Fitzharding, a neonatologist at Toronto's Hospital for Sick Children, in describing prematurity and low birth weight, stated that "only a few years ago, fifteen hundred grams of birth weight was a point of viability and then it became one thousand grams; then seven hundred fifty grams; and soon may be as low as five hundred grams. It is her opinion, however, that babies surviving at such low birth weight do not survive as normal."

In her paper prepared for The Coalition for the Prevention of Handicaps, Barbara McElgunn discussed the identification of low birth weight babies and full size neonates with low Apgar scores as an easily identifiable group of at-risk babies to be followed up and have their development monitored. The Apgar assessment must be administered at one and five minutes of life by a trained and uninvolved observer. In this paper, Mrs. McElgunn says that the Apgar assessment should be seen as an extension of fetal monitoring during pregnancy, labor, and birth. She further says that by identifying persistently common factors, not only can at-risk infants be monitored, but obstetrical measures may be better assessed and modified. This would have the long-term effect of reducing not only infant mortality but certainly the incidence of infant morbidity. It seems evident that screening of newborns for brain dysfunction could allow for the earliest and most effective intervention program to begin in order to prevent and minimize developmental disabilities in children.

EXAMPLES OF EARLY INTERVENTION PROGRAMS

In the borough of Scarborough, Ontario, the public health department, through its public health nurses, has been running a neonatal follow-up program providing education for parents, as well as quality nursing care to high-risk infants, and has been assisting families to utilize other community resources as the special needs of these high-risk children become apparent. Their conclusion is that the acceptance of this program by parents has been excellent.

One interesting program is called Project Follow-up. Children involved in this follow-up service are routinely those children who score below five on the five-minute Apgar assessment and those children who have low birth weight for time of gestation as identified by hospital staff. In addition to this, the medical doctors can request this follow-up service for any infant they are concerned about.

The trained outreach worker visits children in their homes and assesses them using the Bayley Scales at six, twelve, and twenty-four months of age. Following these assessments, the outreach worker reports the child's development to the monitoring physician and follows through on appropriate referrals to other agencies in the community. In addition to this, if the child is falling developmentally behind, the worker assists the parents in devising a home-based infant stimulation program. The hospital outreach worker also serves as a liaison for the parents if the child is placed in a day care center, by assisting them in the selection of a day care center and by working with center staff on an individualized developmental program for these children. The outreach worker follows the child until the time of school entrance and meets with school officials to discuss the development of the child from the time of birth to the time of school entrance.

Project Follow-up has been in operation since October, 1978, and in a recent follow-up survey of parents who have been involved in the program, there was not one negative comment regarding the program.

A similar program was established with the assistance of a government grant, and serves the medical practitioners and parents in a rural community. Evaluations of all of these programs would indicate that parents are extremely appreciative of this assistance and could benefit by more frequent visits from a "home trainer" and more specialized child care services in the community.

RECOMMENDATIONS FOR GOVERNMENT ACTION

In a recent submission to the Canadian Government Task Force on Child Care, the authors of this book summarized the fact that in recent years, many schemes have been attempted in many places, all of which have met with a limited amount of success. The authors feel that this Task Force should make wider, broader, sweeping recommendations and establish a system that would include the following features:

- The earliest possible identification of children who are considered "at risk."
- Regular, periodic follow-up and evaluation of the development of these "at-risk" children.
- If these children, on the developmental tasks, fall in the lowest twenty-fifth percentile of standard measures, direct home service should be offered to assist the parents in establishing goals, providing adequate stimulation, and in task analysis to assist their child in maximizing his/her potential.
- In addition to these services to parents, referral services should be offered and available to general practitioners, pediatricians, and other professionals in the communities as a place to refer children whose development is questionable.
- These developmentally delayed children should have the opportunity to be enrolled in appropriate day care facilities where they can be integrated with their peers and also receive stimulation under the direction of trained professionals to move them toward more normal development.
- During the year prior to school entrance, these children should be made known to the schools that will receive them so that appropriate plans and programs can be established for their benefit and that appropriate support services can be arranged for the teachers who will be receiving them in schools.

This paper concludes that research clearly points out that the earlier periods of a child's development are critical and have a determining effect on later development.

It is only logical therefore to assume that in light of the current knowledge base, we must, as a society, become involved in assisting these children in their readiness to participate in the mainstream of school and adult life. Assisting children with special needs is always a difficult task. However, every dollar that is invested in a three-year-old seems to bring better results than ten dollars invested in an eighteen-or twenty-year-old in assisting them to reach their maximum potential. The following story, taken from *Teaching Exceptional Children*, best illustrates how a direct home service program can assist developmentally delayed children and their parents. (From "Home Based Early Intervention: The Story of Susan," by Davon Gray, *Teaching Exceptional Children*, Volume 12, 1980, pages 79-81. Copyright 1980 by The Council for Exceptional Children. Reprinted with permission.)

A CASE STUDY: THE STORY OF SUSAN

Case History

Susan, an attractive two-and-a-half-year-old with red curly hair and blue eyes, was the youngest of five children. Her mother described Susan as a term baby, but one who was "almost miscarried." According to her mother, Susan's right lung was not functioning well at birth and she was kept in an incubator for two to three days (the mother was unsure of the time). Susan was subsequently diagnosed as having cerebral palsy with residual right hemiplegia.

Susan had been very difficult to care for since birth. She cried excessively day and night, had poor eating and sleeping habits, and was given sleeping medications since shortly after birth. Her mother was extremely protective of Susan, had rarely separated from the child, and carried her in her arms most of each day (even when talking on the phone).

Susan's mother reported placing her, as an infant, in a "home" offering care for severely handicapped children. This placement, however, was only short-term. Before initial program intervention with the family, the parents had contacted the Department of Public Welfare regarding Susan's possible placement in a foster home, although this was never followed up. The program received a referral regarding the family from a nearby clinic and local physician because it was feared Susan might be abused unless there was intervention with the family. The referring clinic found no evidence of physical abuse and the Family Consultant later confirmed the belief that no physical abuse had taken place. Susan's mother was under medical care for "nerves" when the family first entered the program.

INTERVENTION AND PROGRESS

The first visit to the family home left the following impression. The family lived in a small, clean, three-bedroom wooden home, devoid of all table decorations, toys, and books. Everything appeared to be out of reach and out of sight. The house was dark and gloomy, with all lights and lamps turned off and all curtains and blinds drawn, which created a depressing atmosphere. The mother was sitting in a corner of the small living room with Susan on her lap. Throughout the initial visit Susan remained clinging to her mother while continually whining or crying. Susan's eyes appeared to be excessively swollen and her face contorted from what seemed to be continuous crying behavior. Her mother reported that it was this clinging and crying behavior that had led to her request for foster home placement. She spoke of Susan as if she were a severely handicapped child, calling her "that poor little thing." As soon as rapport was established with Susan, initial developmental assessment was obtained using the Birth-3 Developmental Scale (Bangs & Garrett, 1975). The results are shown in Table 1.

Susan's language skills consisted of one word — mama — and much crying and whining accompanied by a few gestures. Hearing was grossly assessed by Susan's reaction to noise, and was thought to be within normal limits. Her mother expressed no concern regarding her hearing. Susan's cerebral palsy seemed to manifest itself largely in the positioning of her right arm and in her limping gait, but did not appear to physically encumber her ability to verbalize.

TABLE 1

**Susan's Initial Assessment versus 2-Month Follow-up
on the Birth-3 Developmental Scale**

	Initial Assessment/Months	2-Month Follow-up Assessment/Months
Chronological Age	32	34
Language		
Comprehension Age	18	24
Language Expression Age	12	18
Problem Solving Age	18	24
Motor Age	18	24
Social Expression Age	24	30

Initial Goals

The initial goals for Susan and her mother were outlined as follows:

1. Work toward gradual physical separation of mother and child.
   a. Short term — Mother and older siblings to leave the house for at least 1 hour.
   b. Long term — Mother to be able to leave home and return without immediately picking Susan up.

2. Shape and reinforce Susan's behavior to extinguish crying.
   a. Short term — Susan to be able to spend part of a therapy session without crying.
   b. Long term — Susan to be able to say "goodbye" upon mother's leaving home and to greet her upon return without crying.

3. Shape and reinforce mother's behavior regarding enrichment of the home environment.
   a. Short term — Some lights should be on at least in the living room, where Susan usually stayed.
   b. Long term — Mother to provide toys and manipulative items for entertainment and enrichment for Susan and her siblings. Mother to open house so sunshine can come in and family can see outside.

4. As soon as behavior is controlled, stimulate and reinforce developmental language program as outlined by the consultant, a certified speech pathologist.

a. Short term — Reinforce babbling and jargon as it emerges.

b. Long term — Stimulate and reinforce language recognition and expression as it emerges initially in single words found in Susan's environment, such as cup, puppy, baby, ball, etc.

c. Counsel family regarding the need to reinforce verbalization in the home, and not to allow gesturing for total communication.

During the first two home visits no attempt was made to separate Susan and her mother. On the third visit, after Susan's mother had indicated trust in the consultant, she agreed to leave the house for a period of no longer than one hour. The Family Consultant found herself with an angry, frightened, and screaming child. Therapy focused on establishing rapport and mutual acceptance with Susan. Because Susan's mother could not drive and knew very few neighbors, she and Mary, Susan's four-year-old sister, merely retreated to the back yard and sat. Until this time, Susan and her mother had reportedly never left the house except for visits to the doctor. As time progressed, the mother was successful in contacting a few neighbors and initiating some socialization without focusing on Susan and her "problems."

Within one month, progress was well established for goals 3 (reinforcing mother's behavior regarding enrichment of home environment) and 4 (stimulation and reinforcement of language development). Progress notes for that day included:

Susan is definitely exhibiting more babbling and jargon, up to five minutes of continuous verbalization with noted inflection and expression, as in conversation, with this consultant. The home is much brighter and much more stimulating than in initial visits. The family has purchased a bright green rug for the floor, and the lights are on upon arrival. There are numerous toys in the room. The efforts of Susan's mother are noted and rewarded verbally.

The use and nonuse of toys in the home is an interesting story in itself. When the Family Consultant asked about toys for Susan, the mother told her there were numerous toys already in the home from the previous children, but she had been afraid Susan would "hurt" herself on them. Later it was discovered that the toys that were brought out at the suggestion of the consultant were put away after the consultant left in the morning. Discussion with Susan's mother remedied this.

Progress on goals 1 (the physical separation of Susan and her mother) and 2 (extinguishing Susan's crying behavior) was slower, but was consistently achieved after about two months of intervention. By that time, arrangements had been made for a high school student, enrolled through her homemaking class as a teacher's aide for the kindergarten and Early Childhood Program, to accompany the Family Consultant to the home. Her role was to interact with Susan's sister. Such activities as arts and crafts, basic cooking experiences, and outdoor picnics with both girls demonstrated to the mother Susan's normalcy and eased the sibling rivalry that was developing between Susan and her sister.

After two months of intervention, progress was assessed using the Birth-3 Developmental Scale (Bangs & Garrett, 1975).

A gain of six months was recorded in a two-month period of intervention in all areas previously assessed.

Working with Susan became particularly interesting during the next period. Susan's environment had previously been very restricted due to her mother's fears that she was a particularly vulnerable child. As a result, she had not been allowed out of her mother's sight or virtually out of her arms. As her experiences were allowed to reflect her growing interests in an unaccustomed, less restricted environment, she demonstrated a particular interest in the family's bathroom. At this point, one of the goals of language therapy was to reinforce any verbalizations, and the bathroom mirror proved exceptionally profitable. We continued to work in the bathroom for a few weeks as interest moved from the mirror to sitting on the toilet (verbalization became quite animated as Susan perched proudly at the previously forbidden height), and finally to playing in the bathtub. In the bathtub setting, initial indications of Susan's imagination and personality were vividly expressed through her modeling play behavior and its accompanying "narrative."

Carryover was noted as both parents reported an increase in verbalization throughout the day, consisting of single words and two-word phrases, as well as attempts to sing along with the television commercials. It was felt that therapeutic language enrichment offered in the child's own home environment had proven stimulating and had served as an easy mode for carryover for the family (i.e., Susan's mother also noted her interest in the bathroom and was also able to successfully elicit verbal responses from her).

Further arrangements were then made for the consultant to accompany Susan to the school district's Early Childhood Program (for ages three to four years). Susan was not enrolled, but joined a group in order to give her experiences in socialization and communication with peers (she was almost three years old at this time). Susan and her sister also attended a neighborhood school program one afternoon a week. Throughout the remainder of the year, Susan was seen two mornings a week in the Early Childhood Program as an observer/participant and three mornings a week in her home. Her mother was routinely asked to join us in an effort to demonstrate Susan's skills and progress, and feedback regarding Susan's activities and progress was also available to the entire family. Contact with Susan's father was minimal, occurring only when evening meetings could be scheduled. However, he did state he had noted and was pleased about Susan's improved speech and behavior.

The following school year Susan was enrolled in the Early Childhood Program. Considering her previous highly restricted environment, it was hoped that Susan's initial year in a school-based program would prove much more rewarding and successful as a result of the home-based early intervention.

Two-Year Follow-up

A two-year follow-up evaluation of Susan was completed at age 5 years, 0 months. Her Early Childhood teacher reported good cooperation and participation at school. A home visit was also made as part of the follow-up assessment. Susan's mother reported that she had good eating and sleeping habits, good family relationships, and greatly increased verbalizations, although she was still frequently difficult to comprehend. The mother did not seem to be as protective and negative as she had been on the initial visit. Susan's older sister was also home during the interview and took pride in helping Susan "show off" her newly acquired skills (e.g. counting blocks, naming household objects, etc.). The Family Consultant had not seen Susan for almost two years. She was impressed with Susan's happy and outgoing personality (in sharp contrast to those initial mornings characterized by dark rooms and a clinging and crying child). Susan's greatest improvement appeared to be in personal and outgoing skills, with language skills continuing to progress slowly. Results of formal language testing at the chronological age of five years included:

1. Houston Test of Language Development, Part II (Crabtree, 1963). Language Age—3 years.

2. Test for Auditory Comprehension of Language (Carrow, 1973). Age Equivalency — 3 years, 1 month.

3. Preschool Language Scale (Zimmerman, Steiner & Evatt). Auditory Comprehension Age — 2 years, 9 months; Verbal Ability Age — 2 years, 5 months.

Although language skills continue to remain delayed, progress is continuing and is encouraging to all members of the family, as well as to the staff at Susan's school. More striking results are noted in the parents' new and positive reports regarding Susan and her ever-improving social interaction.

Summary

This case study of one child and her family illustrates several ways in which a home-based program serves a community. It also illustrates some of the advantages of such a program for some of the more difficult cases.

1. Language stimulation is carried out in a setting familiar to the child and in which he or she will continue to live. Susan's therapy was carried out in the bathroom of her home for several weeks. This was appropriate and also meaningful to her.

2. A home-based program allows the consultant to gather more reliable information concerning self-help skills, parenting, family interactions, and medication regimens.

3. The problem of separation frequently encountered with handicapped children can be dealt with more realistically in the home. Mother and child need to develop the ability to separate at home before the child is left at a nursery school, infant stimulation program, or preschool program.

4. The home-centered program furnishes a viable way for the consultant to gather information when child abuse is suspected.

5. The home-centered program insures that the primary caretaker will participate when the child is seen for therapy. The consultant works not only with the child but with the parents.

6. Parents who are not willing to participate in a facility-centered program (i.e., infant stimulation program or infant care program held in a community facility) often will participate in a home-centered program. Finances and transportation frequently will keep a mother at home; these are not factors in the home-centered program.

7. In addition to the general benefits, Susan and her family received other benefits from being participants. Close liaison with child welfare and the public school's Early Childhood Program prevented the family from having to deal with multiple professionals, each trying to help and to offer duplicating services. Susan received language stimulation from a professional as well as from her mother, guided by the professional, at a critical time for speech and language development.

Infant programs carried out in centers meet many needs, but they often do not afford the opportunity of working with child and mother in their home. Since the mother or mother surrogate has the greatest influence in shaping a child's development and she will be in the home, it seems logical to work with both child and mother in "their natural settings."

PARENT EDUCATION PROGRAMS

Early identification and home-based intervention programs are certainly not the only forms of prevention that can be done within communities. Parents of children not identified as being at risk also need many supports. Traditionally, parenting practices tend to be based on cultural and familial practices rather than on a knowledge base well grounded in research. Dr. Burton White, author of *The First Three Years of Life*, and founder of the Center for Parent Education, firmly believes that, with support and understanding, most parents have the capability of being excellent teachers of their own infants and toddlers. Dr. White's research clearly indicates that there are seven definite stages that all children go through between birth and 36 months of age. He contends that parents should be prepared for each of these stages and should receive information and assistance in dealing with the problems inherent at each stage. Dr. White conludes that the areas of child development most at risk in the young child are:

- language development;
- social competency;
- development of curiosity;
- the roots of intelligence.

These dimensions of development are at risk because of three primary factors: ignorance, stress, and lack of assistance.

Parent education then should be considered an integral part of a preventative program. School boards, along with other community agencies such as public health, social services, mental health centers, and early childhood service providers in day care centers and nursery schools, should cooperate and design a variety of ways to assist parents. Parents need assistance in receiving the most accurate information concerning child development and support to help them cope with the stress that can result from raising children. These programs should stress practical suggestions and offer help in coping with the unique aspects of each phase in child development, with a major emphasis on developing the normal child to the maximum of his potential.

HEARING LOSS AND LANGUAGE DEVELOPMENT

In addition to the emphasis on normal development, parents in a Parent Education Program are alerted to factors that could have a negative effect upon their child's development. For example: making sure that their young children have a hearing assessment. To quote Dr. Burton White, "It is considerably more difficult to grow up to be a fully developed human being if your hearing is impaired during your first years of life. The ability to acquire language is directly dependent upon the ability to hear well. Children undergo rapid basic language learning during the first three years of life. Deficits in language development in three-year-olds are perhaps the most commonly discovered important educational difficulty in underachieving preschool children.

For an older child, or a young adult, a moderate hearing loss constitutes a relatively minor problem. Previous learning allows such people to fill in some of what is not heard clearly. In contrast, when language is being learned for the first time, even minor losses constitute significant obstacles to good development."

HIGH-RISK FACTORS FOR HEARING LOSS

Dr. White and other experts in the field believe that the detection of early hearing loss is possible from four months of age on and parents can be taught to be observant and determine if their child orients to both loud and soft sounds accurately. Experts recommend that if possible, an examination by a pediatric audiologist be done when the child is between four and six months

of age. These procedures are extremely important for those children who might
be high-risk for any of the following reasons:

- Is there a history of hearing loss in the family?
- Has the pregnant woman been exposed to German measles?
- Was the child premature or at a very low birth weight?
- Was there a blood incompatibility problem?
- Has the baby been given Mycin drugs?

Answers to these questions can alert parents to a possible hearing loss
in their children. They can then work with professionals to plan appropriate
support programs.

ASSISTING PARENTS OF PRESCHOOL CHILDREN

Several formats of programs tailored to individual communities have been
developed and offered in a variety of school districts to parents of young children
to assist them in maximizing their child's potential. These programs are offered
to parents of children one year or younger in age and emphasize factual
information, practical suggestions, and a great deal of discussion among the
parents taking the program.

Parent education programs should be designed to assist the parents in
relieving anxiety about being good parents and to assist them in enjoying
the growth and development of their children. One excellent resource that
is particularly helpful is the book, *Loving and Learning: Interacting with Your
Child from Birth to Three*. This book contains many concrete and positive
suggestions for enjoying your child and also on how to utilize materials found
around the house to assist children in their development.

In most communities, particularly in rural areas, school systems employ
the individuals most knowledgeable about child development and early
childhood programming. If a school board firmly believes in a preventative
model for Special Education and wishes to eliminate unnecessary Special
Education programs, as well as to maximize the functioning of those children
requiring special programs, it must offer its support to the staff of day care
centers and nursery schools in its district. This assistance should be both in
program consultation and assessment and programming of "special needs"
children who are enrolled in these settings.

If a school board has adopted a philosophy of mainstreaming, then it is
important that children in local day care centers and nursery schools also
be mainstreamed rather than segregated. This is necessary so that the child's
earliest social and educational contacts outside of the home place her/him
in an integrated program with similar expectations as their nondisabled peers.
Many owners and operators of day care centers and nursery schools will be
frightened and threatened by their initial experiences with integration just
as are many classroom teachers in schools.

If integrated day care and nursery school programs are to be successful, then these individuals will need the support and expertise that can be offered to them by school board personnel.

The final area of the preventative approach to Special Education is preschool screening; because of its importance and direct association to children's initial school experiences, this will be dealt with in detail in the following chapter. Preschool screening of some type is accepted almost universally throughout North America and the role of the school in this screening has much wider acceptance than in the programs dealt with previously in this chapter. Certainly, the variety of programs discussed will take a great deal of time, effort, commitment, and dedication, from those individuals interested in instituting any or all of them. However, the benefits to children and the gratitude of parents supported by these programs easily justify the time and effort involved.

CHAPTER 2 REFERENCE MATERIALS

Barnes, David B., *The Bigger They Are, the Harder*, Submission to Federal Government Task Force, October, 1984.

Address: Dr. David Barnes
      Bennington-Rutland Supervisory Union
      P.O. Box 580
      Manchester Center, VT 05255

Gray, Davon, "Home Based Early Intervention: The Story of Susan," *Teaching Exceptional Children*, Vol. 12, Pages 79-81, Reston VA, 1980.

Address: C.E.C.
      1920 Association Drive
      Reston, VA 22091

McDiarmid; Peterson; and Sutherland, *Loving and Learning: Interactions with Your Child from Birth to Three*, Harcourt Brace Jovanovich, San Diego, CA, 1975.

Address: Harcourt Brace Jovanovich
      1250 Sixth Avenue
      San Diego, CA 92101

McElgunn, Barbara, "Prevention of Handicaps."

Address: Canadian Neurological Coalition
      Suite 126, 100 College Street
      Toronto, Ontario M5G 1L5

Taylor, Bernadette, "Project Follow-Up," Hospital Outreach Worker.

Address: St. Rita Hospital
      490 Kings Road
      Sydney, Nova Scotia B1S 1B4

White, Burton, *The First Three Years of Life*, Prentice-Hall, Inc., Englewood Cliffs, NJ, 1975.

Address: Prentice-Hall, Inc.
      Englewood Cliffs, NJ 07632

The Why and How
of Preschool Screening

---

*Remember always that you have not only the right
to be an individual;
you have an obligation to be one.
You cannot make any useful contribution in this life
unless you do this.*

Eleanor Roosevelt

Preschool screening is certainly an integral part of the preventative approach to Special Education. In the past, it was considered to be early identification, but today, preschool screening must be considered an opportunity to better understand each child in order to prevent school failure. Preschool screening, of course, has been around for a long time, at a variety of levels — some very simple, others very detailed and complex.

Preschool screening, like any other program, can have tremendous advantages for children; but it also has the potential of being totally misused or used for the benefit of teachers and administrators rather than for children. For example, preschool screening has been used to place labels on children and emphasize their weak points rather than their strengths, and has been used to stream children into higher-and lower-functioning classrooms. When properly approached, screening can assist teachers and parents to better understand a child and his/her strengths, weaknesses, and particular learning styles. Only too often, in many school districts, the emphasis around a screening program is on the screening itself, with little thought given to individualizing instruction and programming based on the data collected during the screening.Well designed preschool screening programs assess a wide variety of functional levels in children and have a plan to effectively utilize children's strengths and weaknesses when they begin their school programs. Many programs have utilized the information to design specific learning centers within classrooms and also to train both student and parent volunteers to conduct a wide variety of small group activities within classrooms. Many creative teachers utilizing preschool screening information have designed multimodal methods of presenting major concepts to be learned during the first year of school so that all concepts are approached through the child's learning strength. A general follow-up evaluation by teachers and specialists indicate the following advantages of such classroom organizational patterns:

- a happier child;
- a more confident and more independent child;
- a child more prepared to engage in formalized reading instruction;
- a better informed parent more willing to cooperate with the school in assisting the child with his/her learning program;
- a more satisfied and successful teaching staff;
- more interaction between professionals, teachers, physical education teachers, resource teachers, speech and language therapists, and principals.

TYPES OF PRESCHOOL SCREENING

It is not the intent of the authors to devote this chapter to any specific detailed enumeration of the types of screens to be utilized in any preschool screening, but rather to deal with the purposes of preschool screening and some administrative and operational guidelines that have proven to be helpful.

There are many fine screening programs on the market and also many fine screening programs which have been designed by individual school systems. One such program has been operational in Muncie, Indiana, since 1968. The program has recently become commercialized and computerized, thereby utilizing modern technology to process the results of screening and to develop both home and classroom programs for each individual child as well as suggesting classroom groupings for specific activities for teachers. This program is called the "Insight Unlimited Educational Management Program." Like all good screening programs, it screens motor processing, visual processing, auditory processing, language, and basic concepts. Its great advantage is the timesaving feature of computerized report writing and programming. It conveniently lists students in each class who have strengths in a particular area screened and also those students who have needs in those areas. This format is of great assistance to the classroom teacher in planning his/her program to best meet the needs of the children in the class.

In addition to this, each student screened has a suggested program developed. Following the screening, student's strengths, needs, and suggested activities to be done at home and in the classroom are listed. It is to be hoped that this type of information and teamwork between home and school can be utilized to benefit many children. Figures 3-1 and 3-2 are examples of these reports.

UTILIZING THE SCREENING INFORMATION

Many school systems do detailed screening without using computerized programming, and with staff time and effort, these programs can be extremely valuable and can come up with similar information to assist both parents and teachers in a better understanding of the children. The bottom line with any type of screening or assessment must be the assistance given to the children screened in their areas of need and the utilization of their strengths to have them accomplish required goals.

One example of how this can be done is outlined in a document entitled, "Helpful Hints for Parents: Readiness for School Begins at Home." This document, developed by one of the authors, is useful in that it gives parents many ideas for activities designed to assist their children with school readiness. Following screening, many of these areas of developmental readiness can be further explained to parents. Those areas where a child needs many experiences can be placed in order of priority, when discussing with parents the information from the screening sessions. Many parts of this were not designed with expectations that all parents would do all of these activities with their children, but that they would do those activities most needed by their own child prior to school entrance.

HELPFUL HINTS FOR PARENTS: READINESS FOR SCHOOL BEGINS AT HOME

Learning occurs when talking, looking, playing, listening, jumping, exploring, dancing, creating, singing, skipping, sharing, helping.

How Parents Can Help Before the Child Starts School

1. Take him/her places and show him/her things. Trips to stores, parks, farms, etc., will help him/her know and understand the things he will read about. Allow him to feel, smell, touch, listen, and talk about everything.

2. Answer his questions; give him descriptions and explanations.

3. Help him to speak plainly and distinctly. Give him a good example and encourage him to follow. Be interested in his conversations and stories.

4. Surround him with good books, read to him often, and let him see you reading.

SAMPLE TOTAL CLASS SCREENING REPORT FOR TEACHER

Student Need/Strength Report

DATE: SCHOOL NO.   W001   LEVEL   01

DISTRICT   A002

TEACHER NO.   001   GRADE

STUDENTS WITH STRENGTHS	STUDENTS WITH NEEDS

CAT. 42.0   AUDITORY MEMORY

Debbie Ackers	David Allen
Betty Bailey	Francis Farley
Charlotte Caldwell	
Donald Dunn	
Ernie Evans	
Gretta Green	
Amy Landis	

CAT. 43.0   AUDITORY MEMORY/MOTOR SEQUENCING

Betty Bailey	Francis Farley
Charlotte Caldwell	
Donald Dunn	
Ernie Evans	
Gretta Green	
Amy Landis	

CAT. 45.0   AUDITORY FIGURE GROUND

Betty Bailey	
Charlotte Caldwell	
Donald Dunn	
Ernie Evans	
Francis Farley	
Gretta Green	
Amy Landis	

```
CAT. 46.0          ARTICULATION

                              Debbie Ackers

                              David Allen

                              Betty Bailey

                              Charlotte Caldwell
```

FIGURE 3-1

SAMPLE INDIVIDUAL STUDENT SCREENING REPORT

STUDENT ID# AC-KD102377   INSIGHT UNLIMITED INC.

E.   It appears that your child has learning strengths in these categories:

-4.0-   MOTOR MEMORY SEQUENCING

MOTOR MEMORY SEQUENCING refers to the student's ability to listen to a series of commands, remember them, and perform the activities in the order given. Skill in this area is required when parents or teachers direct the student to carry out instructions requiring motor (muscle) movement. For example, the student may be told, "Clean up your room, empty your wastebasket, hang up your clothes, and make your bed."

-23.0-   POSITION IN SPACE

POSITION IN SPACE refers to the student's ability to recognize the positions of objects in relationship to one another. This includes the student's ability to discriminate between objects or designs that are alike in form, but are turned differently in space. An example of this includes the lower case form of the letters B, D, P, and Q. These letters are alike in "form" (each contains a circle and a straight line) but are different in how the circle and line unite to form the letters. The same concept applies to words. The student may confuse the words "saw" and "was" if he/she is unsure of the positioning of the letters.

-34.0-   CLASSIFICATION

CLASSIFICATION refers to the student's ability to recognize class or category (objects with similar identities), to classify common objects, and to use these objects in order to make logical relationships. Many classroom activities require that the student understand basic methods for categorizing objects or concepts and apply this knowledge in order to facilitate the learning process.

-35.0- REPEAT A PATTERN

REPEAT A PATTERN refers to the student's ability to see, identify, and then copy a block pattern. These skills are essential for the student to later be able to determine the spatial relationships of the circles and lines that unite to form letters of the alphabet, to recognize the forms of those letter symbols, and then be able to reproduce them.

-48.0- EXPRESSIVE VOCABULARY

A student develops an expressive vocabulary in conjunction with her/his imagination. EXPRESSIVE VOCABULARY is the correct usage of words in written and verbal expression. The student must first understand the meanings of words before being able to use those words correctly in speaking or writing. Object naming, counting, giving directions, story telling, and writing are a few of the ways students express vocabulary. The quality or depth of her/his vocabulary is more important than the number of words she/he knows.

F.   It appears that your child needs help within these categories:

-21.0-	VISUAL MEMORY	-28.0-	VISUAL SEQUENCING
-31.0-	FORM LETTER/WORD RECOGNITION	-32.0-	MATHEMATICAL PROCESSES
-46.0-	ARTICULATION	-50.0-	EXPRESSIVE SYNTAX

G.   The first three things you can do at home in each category with your child —

Appropriateness of activities within a code category must be determined by those administering the recommended activities and should be adapted for presentation in the manner most appropriate to the physical, mental, and/or emotional ability of the student.

The student may be "moved through" any activity or have the activity demonstrated to ensure that the instructions are understood and that the activity is being presented at the student's level.

PARENT AWARENESS DATE

-17.0- DOMINANT HAND AND EYE

EXPLANATION/RELATIONSHIP TO LEARNING:

The appreciation of an inner awareness of unilateral dominance (preference) of hand, eye, foot, and ear is related to the development of awareness of space outside the body: how far left or right an object is from the body, as well as where objects are in relation to other objects: Up-down, right-left, and here-there. Awareness of space outside the body is an important factor in the ease or difficulty the student may have in learning how to read, write, speak, and understand concepts.

1. Do not encourage student to switch his/her preferred use of hand, foot, or eye.
2. Cross dominance may require adaptation of the tasks presented to the student in school and at home.
3. Appropriate equipment and location in learning situations are recommended (left-handed scissors and chairs, "elbow room," seating student on extreme right side or left of room, etc.).

NO. OF ATTEMPTS

DATE ACCOMPLISHED

-21.0-   VISUAL MEMORY

EXPLANATION/RELATIONSHIP TO LEARNING:

Visual memory relates to the student's ability to remember objects previously seen. In the area of spelling, it is necessary for the student to be able to remember a visual pattern of letters in order to form words. The same skill is needed when reading. Students who have difficulty in this category may have to continually relearn the spelling of words as well as their relationship to the rest of the words in a given sentence.

1. TOY DESCRIPTION: Use one of the student's toys. Show it to him/her. Remove the toy and ask the student to describe it.
2. LITTLE TOYS: Place a variety of toys on a table. (Use three to start.) The student is shown the toys, then covers her/his eyes while one toy is removed. Students tell which one is missing.
3. PLASTIC GEOMETRIC FORM: Use plastic geometric forms of various shapes, sizes, and colors. Place three in front of the student. After she/he has looked at them, remove them. Ask her/him to tell what they were and the color, if possible.

FIGURE 3-2

5. Don't attempt the job of teaching him to read or manipulate numerals.

6. Help him in selecting his TV programs. This is a good medium for learning if used properly.

7. Be sure your child is physically fit. (A checkup by the doctor will help you in making this decision with special attention to vision and hearing.)

Before Entering School It Is Helpful If Your Child Can Do the Following:

1. State his complete name (possibly address and telephone number, if easily learned).

2. State his father's (mother's) name.

3. Stay in school without mother. (Try a visit with a friend for a day without mother.)

4. Play with a small group of other children.

5. Share playthings with others and wait his turn.

6. Use the bathroom independently. (Flushing toilets, washing hands after, etc.)

7. Fasten his own rubbers and outer garments.

8. If he can tie his own shoelaces, it is a help in the classroom. Encourage it but don't force it.

9. Label all clothing that the child removes in school (sneakers, jackets, boots, coats, etc.).

How Parents Can Help After the Child Starts School

1. Have suitable clothing for all kinds of weather; rubber boots for rainy days, warm clothing and mittens, etc. (Beware of cumbersome fasteners on clothing and boots.)

2. It is important that your child starts off the day with a good breakfast and brings a nourishing snack for his morning break.

3. Encourage bringing home his papers (work at school) and let him tell you all about them. Be careful not to discourage either his efforts or confidence.

4. If possible, try to establish a reading time with your child. Read to him and have as many good picture books and story books as possible available. (Bookmobile service is provided in this area.)

5. Form the habit of sending a note with your child after any absence. It is an important habit and will be of great help to the teacher.

6. A good night's rest is of utmost importance to your child's learning in school. (ten hours)

7. Encourage your child to tell you about the things that happen to him in school. He will like school and you will be happy because he is happy.

Helpful Activities for Your Child

1. Throwing, bouncing, catching balls beginning with a large one and working gradually to smaller ones. Target throwing is fun, too.
2. Make good use of playground equipment for crawling, balancing, climbing, etc. (both frontwards and backwards).
3. Encourage active games with skipping, dancing, jumping, hopping, galloping, running, rolling, lifting, pulling, pushing, tiptoeing, stomping.
4. Provide puzzles and materials requiring skilled use of the hands. (Remember, though, he is only five.)
5. Identifying body parts (e.g., wrist, ankle, elbow).

Body Image

The feeling one has about his own body from his own experiences. A positive body image is developed when the child can identify his body parts and become aware of them and their movements.

Activities

1. Use a full-length mirror to help the child identify the parts of his body. Ask him to touch his head, eyes, knees, elbows, hips, ankles, ears, etc.
2. Ask him to touch the body parts of someone else as you name the parts.
3. Play the game "Simon Says" showing the child what to do.
4. Child points out and names body parts in self-photograph.
5. Functional description — ask questions like: "What do you do with your legs, arms, ears, eyes, etc."
6. Doll play — child can locate doll parts and dress doll.
7. When bathing, encourage the child to look at himself. For example, you may say "Rub soap on your arms, now soap your toes," etc.
8. When dressing, encourage the child to name the parts he or she is covering.
9. Play games such as: "Touch your shoulder, touch the table with your nose, touch the wall with your back," etc.
10. Direct child to place bean bag on the named body parts (may be best done when lying down).

Laterality

Awareness of the two sides of the body and the ability to identify them as left and right.

1. Have the child put on his right shoe first each morning for many days until he has learned the meaning. Then do the same with the left shoe.
2. Have the child lie on the floor and move the arms so that they feel the floor. Also move the legs. (Move left arm sideways, etc.) Raise arms and legs; move right leg.
3. Encourage the child to set the table, especially positioning the cutlery.
4. Give the child directions such as: "Bring me the towel on the right side of the towel rack."
5. Games: "Hokey Pokey," "Simon Says."
6. Move to music — have the child jump on the left foot, jump on the right foot.
7. Remove the shoelaces from a pair of shoes. Have the child put the shoelaces back in the shoes.
8. Play sorting games. For example, ask the child to put all the cars on the right side of him and all the spoons on the left side of him.
9. Marching is good for left-right awareness.
10. Note: If your child is left-handed begin teaching the left side first. If your child is right-handed, begin teaching the right side first.

Static Balance

Balancing when the body is not in motion.

1. Balance on one foot.
2. Balance on one foot with the other as high as the knee.
3. Balance on one foot with the other foot held in various positions.
4. Stand on tiptoes, with eyes opened.
5. Stand on one foot with eyes closed.
6. Have the child stand with feet together and rotate the body from the waist up.
7. Have the child sway back and forth as far as possible without losing balance.
8. Have the child balance and try to kick a ball.
9. Have the child stand on one foot while swinging the other leg.

Gross Motor Jumping

Control of the large muscles of the body. Used for walking, running, skipping, and so forth.

Activities

1. Walk up and down stairs without support other than the feet.

2. Walk like different animals — elephant, ducks, rabbits, cats, etc.

3. Run without going anywhere.

4. Encourage your child to jump on two feet, then one foot.

5. Have your child step and then hop. (This will later turn into a skip.)

6. Encourage your child to play out of doors where there is plenty of room to walk, jump, skip, hop, etc.

7. Roll down slopes.

8. Encourage your child to climb, hang, and slide *whenever possible.*

9. Have your child "draw" big letters in the air with different body parts — arms, legs, head, trunk, etc.

10. Encourage your child (boys especially) to skip a rope.

Recall

The ability to remember what one has learned or experienced.

Children's Activities

1. Card games are fun and teach so much to children.

2. Read the child a story, then ask him to tell you what happened.

3. Teach simple nursery rhymes, songs, riddles, etc.

4. Game — called Memory.

5. Place three objects in front of child, have him hide his eyes then add another object. Ask child to tell you what has been added.

6. Give child simple directions to follow such as, "Pick up your red car and put it on the table."

7. Some children enjoy repeating television commercials.

8. Clap a simple pattern with your hands such as — clap, clap, clap. Have child repeat. (A drum can also be used.)

9. In the evening talk about the events of the day such as: "What did you have for lunch?"

10. Spelling child's name for memory.

Dynamic Balance

This involves the balancing of the body when it is in motion.

1. Have the child walk along a narrow board.

2. Have the child walk a narrow line forward, backward, sideways without stepping off.

3. Have the child walk a line with an eraser on the palm of each hand.

4. Have the child jump along a line.

5. Have the child walk barefoot along a stretched-out skipping rope without stepping off. Go forward, backward, sideways.

6. Put objects along the rope and have the child step over them.

7. Put objects along the rope and have the child pick them up as he moves along the rope.

8. Move marbles, in a spoon, from one container to another across a distance of 10 to 12 feet.

9. Walk about the room with a book on the head.

10. Walk about the room stepping over objects, still with a book on the head.

Space and Directions

Whole-body movements in relation to space.

Activities

1. Have the child crawl under, over, in, through some objects in the house.

2. Have the child step in, on, out of, up on, down from, over objects. Also have him climb on, up, or down, etc.

3. Have the child walk around the table, stand behind it, in front of it, sit on the edge of it, etc.

4. If your child has blocks, direct him or her to do some activities such as:
   - Put small blocks together.
   - Put a red block on a blue block.
   - Put a large block on a small block, etc.

5. With objects of various sizes:
   - Bring the object close to you.
   - Put the object far away.
   - Put the object on the left.
   - Put the object on the right, etc.

6. When outside, allow the child to crawl over, under, and through fences or large cracks.

7. Play follow the leader in the water when at the beach. Leap over the water, duck under the water, jump in, jump out, etc. By giving the child directions, he/she becomes familiar with words and meanings.

8. See if the child can judge the amount of space needed. Example — How wide must I open the door to get through?

9. How close can the child place two objects without having them touch?

10. When preparing for bed, have the child play a game where he or she
    - takes up as little space as possible.
    - takes up as long a space as possible.
    - takes up as wide a space as possible.

Eye-Hand Coordination

The development of skills with the hands and feet. These skills are needed before printing. Hands and eyes must work together in these simple activities.

Activities

1. Bounce a ball back and forth to the child. (A large light ball is recommended rather than a small heavy ball.)
2. Throw the ball overhand to the child.
3. Throw the ball underhand to the child.
4. Game — Use an empty waste basket and let the child throw the ball in the basket. Move the basket further away as the child improves.
5. Let the child kick the ball back and forth to you with his feet.
6. Tear newspaper pieces into shapes such as cats, rabbits, etc.
7. Pasting, coloring, cutting activities.
8. Playing with blocks, rig a jig, sandbox with containers, etc.
9. Putting money in a piggy bank; painting with finger paint is especially good.
10. Playing with clay or modeling compound is excellent for developing the fine muscles of the hand.

Color

Children can often distinguish one color from another, but need to be able to name the colors as well.

Activities

1. Have him pick out his clothing rather than handing him the clothes. Tell him, "Put on your blue shirt."
2. Sesame Street.
3. Have child identify colors on the labels of canned goods, dishes, etc.
4. Encourage child to draw with large primary crayons and tell you the colors he has used.
5. When driving along, play a game of counting all the red cars, etc. Whoever has counted the most when you arrive home wins the game.
6. When you are taking a walk, have child point out all the yellow things he sees, etc.
7. Have the child find all the things in the room that are red, blue, etc.
8. Give the child a bag with different colored objects. Have the child sort the objects according to color and then name the color.
9. Have child cut pictures from catalogues or magazines that are different colors.
10. It may be fun to make a color book with pictures cut from magazines.

Have child paste all the red things on one page, all the blue on another, etc.

Visual Readiness

Activities

1. Make a game of separating coins, pennies from nickels, etc.
2. Give child an assortment of nuts and bolts to be fitted together.
3. Put simple jigsaw puzzles together.
4. Have child tell you the shapes of objects, such as a circle, square, triangle, diamond, star, heart, etc.
5. Sort buttons according to color, shape, size.
6. Point out varied objects in the house, yard, from the car, and comment on the differences.
7. Arrange four checker patterns — three identical and one slightly different; have child point out the difference. Repeat using sticks, blocks, nails, toys, etc.
8. Arrange a series of animal pictures for the child to point out and describe.
9. Draw a picture of a boy or girl. Then draw an incomplete picture beside it. Ask child to tell you what is missing in the second picture.
10. There are many worthwhile activities found in commercially produced books that can be purchased at discount or department stores. For example, finding the hidden pictures, the differences, likenesses, etc. *Be sure* to select books for appropriate ages.

Number Concept

The counting and understanding of a number of things.

Activities

1. Ask your child to set the table and count the correct number of knives, forks, spoons, etc.
2. Sesame Street has very stimulating ideas.
3. Count blocks, cars, toys.
4. Play simple games requiring moves with one, two, three or more steps, places, etc.
5. Manage small amounts of money.
6. Use terms bigger, smaller, less, half, more.
7. Let child count the number of people at the table, buttons on his coat, objects that he can either touch or see.
8. Ask your child to bring you three clothespins, five pennies, etc. Correct only if he/she is wrong.

9. Plan family activities with him/her; use the clock, calendar to help him/her understand hours, days, weeks, months, years. Also ages, birthdays, growth, and measuring.
10. With an assortment of objects in a bag, ask child to pick out all the cars, blocks, forks, etc. Then count them.

Most of the school systems in North America have some type of screening, either through medical reports by school medical staff, or at least an evaluation of vision and hearing. More detailed screening is certainly desirable, but certain factors should be considered by systems that have not previously been involved with screening.

PREPARING PARENTS FOR PRESCHOOL SCREENING

First and foremost, the parents must be prepared and someone must explain to them that preschool screening is and what it is not. They must be informed and reassured that the screening is being done to assist their child in maximizing his/her potential and to prevent early failure and frustration in the school system. One helpful tool in doing this was a paper prepared for parents and distributed approximately one month prior to the screening days. This paper, entitled "Everything You Wanted to Know About Preschool Screening but Were Afraid to Ask" is in a question and answer format.

EVERYTHING YOU WANTED TO KNOW ABOUT PRESCHOOL SCREENING BUT WERE AFRAID TO ASK

Question 1

What if my child refuses to go through the preschool screening? My child is quite shy in new situations.

Answer

If a child refuses to participate in the screening, he would not be forced. Yet this very information is helpful to us because it may give us an indication of how this child may react to his first day of school. We would recommend more social contact over the summer months.

Question 2

Why are you doing preschool screening?

Answer

We are basically concerned about your child's readiness for school. For example, perhaps your child could benefit from activities which will help develop readiness for paper and pencil tasks which will be required during the coming school year.

Question 3

Why don't you wait until September to screen?

Answer

It Is better to have an idea of each child's readiness for school before school opens because it gives extra time before school begins to help develop readiness skills. It also gives time to make appropriate referrals for vision, speech, and hearing tests if necessary.

Question 4

What do you do with the information gained from the screening?

Answer

The information gathered helps both the parents and the teacher get a clear picture of the child's readiness in different areas of development and which of those areas, if any, will require more development over the summer months. All parents are invited to have the screening results explained by the child's teacher and/or the school principal.

Question 5

Is screening just another name for testing?

Answer

No. In no way are we intending to group children by intelligence. In fact, we are not trying to determine intelligence. We are trying to see how ready for school the child is.

Question 6

Will my child be allowed to go to school if he does poorly on the screening?

Answer

The purpose of the screening is not to keep children out of school but to provide activities that will make them more ready for school.

Question 7

What happens if a child does poorly on the screening?

Answer

We would discuss this with you at the parent meeting and may recommend formalized testing.

Question 8

Do the screening results go on the child's permanent record cards?

Answer

No. Children don't pass or fail the screening. We are not going to label children; we will only try to provide a more meaningful program for them.

Question 9

If my child does poorly on the screening, does that mean he will do poorly in school?

Answer

Doing poorly in the early grades is exactly what we are trying to prevent. By doing this, we hope to prevent children from feeling like failures; which happens when adults expect children to do things that they are developmentally not ready to handle. Giving a child an appropriate readiness program will help to avoid the possibility of that child doing "poorly" in school.

Question 10

Who are these people doing the preschool screening? Are they professionals?

Answer

We do not use professionals for the majority of the screens. Rather, the child will meet the teacher he or she will have as well as people from the community who have volunteered to help the school run the screening. All of these people will try to make the child feel comfortable and happy. Remember, we are *not* testing. We are gathering information to determine needs for school readiness.

THE CHILD-CENTERED APPROACH

In addition to parents being prepared for the screening, it is also important that other professionals in the community are involved in the screening process where possible. Public health nurses have been invaluable in many communities in the screening and have often assisted with the vision and hearing screening, as well as taking developmental history information from parents and giving helpful public health information to parents. One thing must be remembered. The screening day should be a pleasant day for the child and the parents and it is often helpful to design a fun book for the child to take home with him as well as information that will be of help to parents which can include school calendars, general school information, and helpful hints on home activities that assist in school readiness. As mentioned previously, screening is a tool and can be used or misused. We hope that the following fictitious story will illustrate the proper use of information gained and utilized through a screening and programming orientation to prevent school failure.

STORIES OF TWO GRADE TWO STUDENTS

Try to imagine yourself as a child who has just begun Grade Two. You have a developmental lag in the area of visual motor processing. In your first year of school, at least until Christmas, you thought that you were very much loved and a pretty smart little kid. You always know the answers to questions your teacher asked about the stories. But something started to happen after the most beautiful of Christmases in your Grade One year of school. The teacher was becoming more and more angry with you. You couldn't print your name, make your letters, and other such important things. You probably don't remember why you began to feel stupid, but by the time you completed Grade One ... there was no doubt about it ... you really were one of the class dummies. You knew this very well because you couldn't copy from the board and you never finished your work on time. Boy! You were always in trouble. Your Grade One teacher decides that you will not be able to cope with Grade Two work. Let's face it! You didn't hand in one assignment that was readable or finished. It was difficult for all concerned, but the teacher was obligated to tell you that you must repeat Grade One ... *you failed*.

It doesn't seem to bother you that your best buddy won't be sitting beside you next year. Repeating Grade One was very much the same as the year before. You still couldn't get your work done on time, and teacher still couldn't read it, but by some sort of magic formula, you were promoted to Grade Two. Finally, here you are in Grade Two and your teacher feels that you should be tested. A referral is made, and the man with the big black case comes and gives you some tests. He, and the resource teacher decide that your perceptions about yourself are correct. You are too dumb to do real Grade Two work, and so now, you are told that you will go with the resource teacher three times a week for help.

These feelings of failure and inadequacy within our young are the very core of the matter. But what can we do within the system, when you find yourself in an area lacking trained personnel, materials, money, community-based programs, etc. To make an impact, you must first define your philosophy. However, definition alone is not enough. You also need the willingness to give of yourself two precious gifts — time and enthusiasm.

In addition to this, you must develop the ability to look at life through a child's eyes. This is the primary reason for a program or philosophy based on the prevention of failure. It is usually only after failure that labeling occurs. Once again, let's move back in time and relive the story of the child having a developmental lag in the area of visual motor processing.

Try to imagine that ...

You are a preschooler; young. fresh, and interested in life around you, and oh, so curious about going to school. Your first exposure to school will be in the spring when you go to the school building for preschool screening. Your parents have been talking about this, but this big word doesn't mean anything to you.

When you arrive at school on the day of the screening, your mom and dad will sit closely by the edge of the gym while you play some interesting games. You will not realize that the purpose of this session will be an opportunity for your teachers to gather information about your school readiness. Remember, your teachers do not wish to provide you with learning experiences that will make you feel like a failure. They will be interested in:

- how you see and hear;
- how you talk and understand what someone else says;
- how you remember what you see and hear;
- how you move and use your hands;
- whether you know right and left and the parts of your body.

Roughly five to ten percent of you may be referred for more intensive testing following the screening. A closer look may be required because some may be shy or tired and do not perform well on the day of the screening. Your teacher and other interested volunteers and staff will now have a clearer picture of what you are all about.

They will develop a profile sheet that shows your strengths and your areas of need. Following that, your parents will be called back to the school for a feedback of information from the screening and a discussion of your strengths and weaknesses and how they perceive these in relation to things that you do at home. In addition to this, they will be given some suggestions for summer play and learn activities that will be fun for you to do with your parents prior to the opening of school next fall. As a result of this meeting, positive lines of communication will be established between your home and your school so that information can readily and honestly flow back and forth in their efforts to assist you to be the best person you can be.

A short time after your morning at the preschool screening, you begin to notice that your mom or dad would rather play ball with you, instead of encouraging you to watch Sesame Street. Summer passes with more games than usual and you find yourself anxiously awaiting the first day of school. You know deep down that you are loved very much and that you are a pretty smart little kid. You find yourself adjusting to your teacher's expectations and you begin to notice that when the other children are doing paperwork, you go to your special place in the room and play some special games. The games are very often different. Sometimes, you glue macaroni around the edge of a shape, and other times, you trace large circles or make a pretty necklace. After the most beautiful of Christmases in your first school year, you begin to notice that you cannot use paper and pencil as well as the other kids. But it doesn't matter, because you are great at remembering, and the poor little girl who sits next to you can never remember what happens in the stories.

Within the philosophy of prevention and early identification, one can see through the difference in these two stories of a child with the same problem, how the child-centered approach becomes much more important than the curriculum-centered approach. We know that all children do not enter school with the same degree of readiness.

When you consider the two alternatives presented, it becomes apparent that it is much more difficult to program for and help a child who has experienced years of frustration and failure. On the other hand, if a child's needs are considered and dealt with at the appropriate point in time, there will be no need to spend years in remediation.

School systems deciding whether or not to become involved with preschool screening or who are evaluating their screening process, must answer the critical questions of why they are screening and how they are utilizing the information. This is much more important than what they are doing in terms of screening procedures.

CHAPTER 3 REFERENCE MATERIALS

Barnes, Cheryle, "Helpful Hints for Parents: Readiness for School Begins at Home," unpublished.

Barnes, Cheryle, and Parush, Barbara, "Everything You Wanted to Know About Preschool Screening, but Were Afraid to Ask."

Address: Mrs. Cheryle Barnes
              Bennington-Rutland Supervisory Union
              P.O. Box 580
              Manchester Center, VT 05255

"Insight Unlimited Educational Management Program."

Address: Insight Unlimited, Inc.
              3600 East Memorial Drive
              Muncie, IN 47302

Lichtenstein, Robert, and Ireton, Harry, *Preschool Screening: Identifying Young Children with Developmental and Educational Problems*, Grune & Stratton, Inc., Orlando, FL, 1984.

Address: Grune & Stratton, Inc.
              c/o Academic Press
              Orlando, FL 32887

CHAPTER 4

Conducting Educational Assessment

If the only tool,
You have is a hammer,
You tend to see every problem
As a nail.

Abraham Maslow

There have been many fine and detailed books written on assessment of students having school difficulties. It is not the intent of this chapter to suggest what tests should be used in assessing a child but rather to look at the factors that must be assessed, and how these factors can be utilized in developing an individualized program for each student.

FACTORS FOR CONSIDERATION IN STUDENT ASSESSMENT

There are no magic formulas in assessment. Even the weighting of the various factors which should be assessed in designing a program for a child will vary, depending upon the child's amount of need, the age, and the school he or she attends as well as the availability of a variety of options to choose. These factors include the following:

- physical capabilities;
- personal traits;

- socio-economic factors;
- academic potential in terms of learning strengths and weaknesses;
- acquired skills;
- previous education and training programs;
- individual interests;
- leisure time activities;
- adaptive behavior.

SOURCES OF ASSESSMENT DATA

Often assessment means only testing. Too often this testing is utilized for the purpose of placing a diagnostic label rather than on a better understanding of a child, even though a specific program can be set up to assist with his/her schooling.

Although testing certainly is valuable, it should be only one source of data. Other valuable sources of data are:

- parent interviews;
- student interviews;
- teacher observation;
- direct observation by person responsible for assessment;
- analyzing work samples;
- screening and informal assessment procedures.

REFERRAL

One important aspect of assessment that may be overlooked is the approach to referral. Often the individuals whose responsibility it is to carry out assessment and programming do not have a clear picture why the child is being referred because the referring teacher or school does not give enough detailed information. When this is the case, assessment may become merely a routine giving of psychological tests with no real emphasis on analysis and looking at the reason the child was referred. Additional time spent on accurate and specific referral information is extremely valuable and can save a great deal of wasted effort at later stages of both assessment and programming. Referral is often made with only a simple statement that the child cannot keep up or cope with the regular curriculum for his or her grade level. Referrals such as this do not give specific details of the behavioral observations made by the teacher in the classroom. These observations may be the best indicators for better understanding the child's learning style and in suggesting programs. In completing a detailed referral form, the teacher begins to get some ideas of solutions or ways of dealing with the child in the classroom even prior to receiving the report of the assessment.

Figure 4-1 is a copy of the precision referral form recommended for use in elementary schools.

FUNCTIONAL AREAS TO BE ASSESSED

Although there are many factors to be analyzed in doing a complete assessment of a student, certainly the physical must be basic. We must understand a child's state of physical functioning. This should of course include assessment of vision, assessment of hearing, and taking into account any specific medical problems.

THE ASSESSMENT OF VISION

The assessment of vision is perhaps especially confusing to educators as they very often suspect vision problems and suggest that parents take their child for a professional eye examination. It is at this point that many different results may happen depending upon the individual the parents have chosen to evaluate their child's vision. Many parents, especially in rural areas, take their child to the family doctor, who does not have the equipment or expertise to completely evaluate visual functioning. In addition to this, there have long been differences among eye specialists as to criteria for prescribing glasses and in treatment of visual difficulties other than acuity.

A complete eye examination should include the following:

- *motility* - the ability of the eye muscles to smoothly direct the eyes;
- *teaming* - the ability of both eyes to work together;
- *vergence* - the ability of the eyes to adjust rapidly from far to near and near to far;
- *near-point acuity* - the clarity of the vision at normal reading distance;
- *far-point acuity* - the ability of the child to see clearly at distance.

A complete visual examination is necessary to enable the student to have the best possible vision skills, and to enable school personnel to understand those children who have visual difficulties and ways in which they may assist them in a classroom setting. The Optometric Extension Program Foundation has published an educator's checklist (see Figure 4-2) to assist teachers in making directed observations that may give clues to children in their classroom having visual difficulties.

Schools should work as closely as possible with the optometrists and ophthalmologists in their community to avoid misunderstandings and to work together for the best possible visual functioning of their students.

THE ASSESSMENT OF HEARING

The ability to hear well certainly is critical to any child's ability to perform well in the school situation, especially with a young child where the classroom

PRECISION REFERRAL FORM

Screening Checklist for Classroom Teachers

Student . . . . Sex . . . .

Date of Birth . . . . Age . . . .

Grade . . . . . . School . . . . Teacher . . . .

Parent/Guardian . . . .

Address . . . . Telephone No. . . . .

Referred by . . . . Date . . . .

Referred to . . . . Date . . . .

DISCREPANCIES
Indicate Positive Assertion by (X)

——— • Performs better in class than indicated by assessment of potential on group IQ tests.

——— • Does not perform as well in class as group IQ tests indicate.

——— • Erratic in performance. Does well at times, poorly at times.

——— • Achievement discrepancy in different subjects; high in one, low in another.

——— • Scores on achievement tests below grade level.

——— • Better on tasks where does not have to verbalize.

——— • Better on tasks where can verbalize.

——— • Better in arithmetic than in reading.

——— • Better in reading than in arithmetic.

——— • Learns reading better by whole word approach.

——— • Learns reading better by phonetic approach.

——— • Cannot learn to read by either whole word or phonetic approach.

—— • Is noisy and disruptive in classroom.

—— • Is so quiet, can forget is in classroom.

—— • Understands spoken instructions better than written instructions.

—— • Understands written instructions better than spoken instructions.

—— • Has difficulty sequencing syllables or letters in speaking and/or reading and/or oral spelling as pasghetti for spaghetti; contustition for constitution; calapillar for caterpillar.

—— • Written spelling slightly superior to oral spelling.

—— • Prefers visual activities (drawing, sports).

—— • Difficulty learning syllabication and accent.

—— • Silent reading better than oral reading.

—— • Comprehension of reading material below reading ability.

VISUAL DIFFICULTIES

—— • Visually confuses letters or words which appear similar, as ram-ran, ship-snip.

—— • Slow to recognize letters as looking the same or different.

—— • Reverses or inverts letters during reading and/or spelling as p-q, c-o, m-w, u-n.

—— • Difficulty learning sequences of letters in reading and/or spelling, as saw-was, stop-spot.

—— • Difficulty retaining visual information such as how pictures or rooms look or what letters and/or numbers look like.

—— • Drawings are inferior and lacking in detail.

—— • Difficulty putting puzzles together or arranging letters.

—— • Does poorer on visual tasks than on auditory tasks.

—— • Prefers auditory activities such as class discussion, story-telling, to less verbal activities.

—— • Does not do well in activities which require reading instructions.

- • Confuses identification of right-left in relationship to own body parts, or own body parts of others, or on pencil-paper assignments, or when moving about the room or a building.

- • Difficulty learning how to tell time.

- • Difficulty learning order of the days of week, or seasons of the year.

- • Inability to read graphs, maps, globes, or floor plans.

- • Difficulty judging distances.

- • Difficulty spacing letters and/or words appropriately.

AUDITORY DIFFICULTIES

- • Formulation and syntax errors in spoken language.

- • Difficulty understanding spoken directions unless they are shortened and simplified.

- • Speech not as clear as should be for age level.

- • Quiet, not talkative.

- • Difficulty "finding" words for speech; substitutes words like "thing," "whatchamacallit" for nouns.

- • Poor vocabulary, especially when questioned for oral definitions.

- • Difficulty or slowness in organizing thoughts for expression.

- • Difficulty retaining directions or information obtained through listening.

- • Uses phrases or single words rather than sentences.

- • Difficulty discriminating consonant sounds; hears mat for bat; tab for tap; betting for bedding.

- • Does not hear rhyming words.

- • Difficulty discriminating and learning short vowel sounds.

- • If given a word has difficulty sounding word out, sound by sound, as "cat" is made up of k-a-t.

- • Cannot pick out initial, middle, or final sounds of words.

- • If given sounds of a word, difficulty knowing what word is (blending k-a-t into cat).

- • Difficulty relating printed letters to their sounds (as "f," "pl," "ide").

62

——— • Cannot separate sounds which make up blends, as "fl" has sounds of f-f-f . . . l-l-l.

——— • Spells and reads sight words more correctly than phonetic words.

KINESTHETIC OR MOTOR DIFFICULTIES

——— • Difficulty imitating gestures, especially face to face.

——— • Difficulty recalling motor patterns used in daily life if objects are not present (e.g., recalling how to move to answer telephone).

——— • Poor coordination for self-help; tying shoes, buttoning, etc.

——— • Poor balance.

——— • Cannot copy appropriate to age because of poor coordination.

——— • Cannot copy appropriate to age for reasons other than poor coordination.

——— • Does poorly on any pencil-paper task or will not attempt these.

——— • Written spelling significantly lower than oral spelling.

——— • Difficulty executing motor patterns for speech resulting in inarticulate or mumbled speech.

——— • Difficulty remembering how to write letters although can remember what they look like.

——— • Difficulty keeping time to music, marching, skipping, cutting.

——— • Cannot stay within lines when coloring.

——— • Poor pencil grasp.

BEHAVIOR SYMPTOMS

——— • Aggressive, irritable, then remorseful.

——— • Impulsive — lacks self control, touches and handles things.

——— • Low tolerance for frustration.

——— • Withdraws — on the outskirts of activities.

——— • Easily excitable, overreacts.

—— ● Erratic behavior. Quick changes of emotional response.

—— ● Hyperactive.

—— ● Hypoactive.

—— ● Unable to concentrate on one activity for long.

—— ● Short attention span compared to peers.

—— ● Pupil can meaningfully relate to others.

—— ● Pupil can predict the consequences of his/her own behavior.

—— ● Easily distracted by noise, color, movement, activity, detail.

—— ● Tendency to become locked in a simple repetitive motor activity.

—— ● Repeats verbally when no longer appropriate (perseverates).

—— ● Pays attention to everything, tends to others' business.

—— ● Disorganized.

—— ● Attention jumps from one thought to another.

—— ● Does better work when shut away from distractions.

—— ● Requires more than usual amount of individual help and attention to learn.

—— ● Dislikes school, especially during reading, writing, or arithmetic periods.

—— ● Cannot complete work independently.

—— ● Very attentive.

OTHER INFORMATION
(use space below)

FIGURE 4-1

EDUCATOR'S CHECKLIST OF
OBSERVABLE CLUES TO CLASSROOM
VISION PROBLEMS

Student's Name ———————————————— Date —————————

1. **APPEARANCE OF EYES:**

   One eye turns in or out at any time ———————

   Reddened eyes or lids ———————

   Eyes tear excessively ———————

   Encrusted eyelids ———————

   Frequent styes on lids ———————

2. **COMPLAINTS WHEN USING EYES AT DESK:**

   Headaches in forehead or temples ———————

   Burning or itching after reading or desk work ———————

   Nausea or dizziness ———————

   Print blurs after reading a short time ———————

3 **BEHAVIORAL SIGNS OF VISUAL PROBLEMS:**

   A. <u>Eye Movement Ability (Ocular Motility)</u>

   Head turns as reads across page ———————

   Loses place often during reading ———————

   Needs finger or marker to keep place ———————

   Displays short attention span in reading or copying ———————

   Too frequently omits words when reading ———————

   Repeatedly omits "small" words ———————

   Writes slanted up or down on paper ———————

   Rereads or skips lines unknowingly ———————

   Orients drawings poorly on page ———————

   B. <u>Eye Teaming Abilities (Binocularity)</u>

   Complains of seeing double (diplopia) ———————

65

Repeats letters within words   ———

Omits letters, numbers or phrases   ———

Misaligns digits in number columns   ———

Squints, closes, or covers one eye   ———

Tilts head extremely while working at desk   ———

Consistently shows gross postural deviations at all desk activities   ———

C. Eye-Hand Coordination Abilities

Must feel objects to assist in any interpretation required   ———

Eyes not used to "steer" hand movements (extreme lack of orientation, placement of words or drawings on page)   ———

Writes crookedly, poorly spaced: cannot stay on ruled lines   ———

Misaligns both horizontal and vertical series of numbers   ———

Uses hand or fingers to keep place on the page   ———

Uses other hand as "spacer" to control spacing and alignment on page   ———

Repeatedly confuses left-right directions   ———

D. Visual Form Perception (Visual Comparison, Visual Imagery, Visualization)

Mistakes words with same or similar beginnings   ———

Fails to recognize same word in next sentence   ———

Reverses letters and/or words in writing and copying   ———

Confuses likenesses and minor differences   ———

Confuses same word in same sentence   ———

Repeatedly confuses similar beginnings and endings of words   ———

Fails to visualize what is read either silently or orally   ———

Whispers to self for reinforcement while reading silently   ———

Returns to "drawing with fingers" to decide likenesses and differences   ———

E. Refractive Status (Nearsightedness, Far-sightedness, Focus Problems, etc.)

Comprehension reduces as reading continues; loses interest too quickly).   ———

Mispronounces similar words as continues reading   ———

Blinks excessively at desk tasks and/or reading;
not elsewhere   ———

Holds book too closely; face too close to desk surface   ———

Avoids all possible near-centered tasks   ———

Complains of discomfort in tasks that demand visual
interpretation   ———

Closes or covers one eye when reading or doing desk work   ———

Makes errors in copying from chalkboard to paper on desk   ———

Makes errors in copying from reference book to notebook   ———

Squints to see chalkboard, or requests to move nearer   ———

Rubs eyes during or after short periods of visual acuity   ———

Fatigues easily; blinks to make chalkboard clear up
after desk task   ———

OBSERVER'S SUGGESTIONS:

Signed: _____

(Encircle):   Teacher;   Nurse;   Remedial Teacher;   Psychologist;

                Vision Consultant;   Other

Address _____

FIGURE 4-2

is basically an auditory situation. When assessing a child who appears to have deficits in his or her language development, it is important not only to ascertain the present level of hearing ability, but (in discussions with parents) to determine if prior to school entry there were periods of time when the child suffered mild to moderate hearing losses.

Dr. Burton White states that: "The ability to acquire language is directly dependent upon the ability to hear well. Children undergo rapid basic language acquisition during the first three years of life. Deficits in language development in three-year-olds are perhaps the most commonly discovered important educational difficulty in underachieving preschool children.

For an older child, or a young adult, a moderate hearing loss constitutes a relatively minor problem. Previous learning allows such people to fill in some of what is not heard clearly. In contrast, when language is being learned for the first time, even minor losses constitute significant obstacles to good development.

It is extremely important that periodic hearing assessments be done on all children. In addition to this, more frequent assessments should be done on children having a history of hearing problems and on children in whom teachers observe a change in behavior or performance within the classroom.

The classroom teacher may often be the first person to suspect that a child is suffering from a hearing loss. The Elks Purple Cross Fund has published a list of symptoms of impaired hearing for teachers to watch for in their classrooms. (See Figure 4-3.)

The symptoms in Figure 4-3 may also at times indicate other difficulties; however, it would be wise to examine them in the light of other information available to you and your colleagues and, where indicated, appropriate assistance should be sought.

When a child with a suspected hearing loss is referred for assessment, the initial screening is usually done by either school system personnel or public health nurses.

The child with problems is then usually examined by a medical doctor. The physician takes a detailed medical history and does a physical examination using an otoscope to view the auditory canal and eardrum. Based on this evaluation the physician may order a complete audiometric evaluation to determine the functional levels of hearing in order to fully diagnose the problems.

AUDIOMETRIC EVALUATION

Complete hearing assessment usually consists of a variety of the following tests:

- *Pure Tone Audiometric Screening* — The child is presented with pure tones over the frequency range of 250Hz through 8000 Hz with the audiometer set at 20 to 25 dB. The child who cannot hear sounds at two or more frequencies is further assessed.

**EDUCATOR'S CHECKLIST OF OBSERVABLE CLUES TO
CLASSROOM HEARING PROBLEMS**

SYMPTOMS OF IMPAIRED HEARING

Physical Symptoms

- frequent earaches
- discharge from the ears
- faulty equilibrium
- complaints of "noise" (ringing, buzzing, hissing) in the child's ears

Speech and Voice Symptoms

- omission of certain sounds in speech
- mispronunciation of common words
- habitually speaking too loudly or too softly

Behavior Reactions in the Classroom

- frequent requests for repetitions of words
- turning of one side of head toward speaker
- inattention during class discussions
- habitually watches speaker's lips
- straining in an attempt to hear
- frequent mistakes in following verbal directions
- appears unaware when spoken to, if not watching the speaker
- inappropriate or irrevelant answers to questions
- frequently watches others before beginning a task and has a tendency to imitate actions of others

Other Signs That May Be Indicative of Impaired Hearing

- poor auditory discrimination ability
- irritability
- child may be more intelligent than his work indicates
- frequent temper tantrums
- a tendency to withdraw "or daydream"

FIGURE 4-3
69

- *Pure Tone Threshold Audiometry* — This is used to determine if the hearing loss is conductive, sensorineural, or mixed. This is accomplished by comparison of air conduction and bone conduction thresholds.

- *Special Audiometric Tests* — These tests are designed for use with very young children and special cases where accurate responses would be impossible to elicit with the more standard tests. They include sound field audiometry, behavioral play audiometry, impedance audiometry, and evoked response audiometry.

HEARING-IMPAIRED CHILDREN IN THE CLASSROOM

If a child has a severe hearing loss, the classroom teacher will usually receive support and a program specifically designed for that child. However, often teachers are given children with mild to moderate hearing losses due to recurrent ear infections. Figure 4-4 is a list of suggestions to assist the teacher in working with these students.

Other aspects of children's physical functioning of course should be investigated and included in the overall composite picture of each child being assessed. However, for the purposes of this book, there are just too many conditions which can have possible effects on the child's ability to adapt to the classroom situation. Educators must rely on medical practitioners for this specific information regarding an individual child. An excellent text by Blackhurst and Berdine discusses many of the most common conditions and is listed at the end of this chapter.

Needless to say, maintaining good relationships between school and parents, and school and medical practitioners in the community is the best possible way to deal with such a variety of physical difficulties that might have negative effects upon a child's level of school performance.

ATTENTION DEFICIT DISORDER

One condition which must, however, be dealt with is Attention Deficit Disorder, which has proven to be an extreme problem for children, their parents, and their teachers, and is diagnosed with or without hyperactivity. One difficulty in dealing with this topic is that it is a relative term and tends to be very much overused.

Some of the difficulty in dealing with children having attentional difficulties is that we are observing a symptom and this symptom may be the result of a variety of causes. It has been the experience of the authors of this book over many years that attentional deficits can be dealt with successfully by a variety of methods. Medication, restrictive diet, and classroom organization have all proven to be very beneficial, both individually and in combination.

In attempting to deal with the attentional deficits with any individual child, often a variety of interventions must be tried. To be most successful

SUGGESTIONS FOR CLASSROOM TEACHERS
WITH HEARING IMPAIRED STUDENTS

- If the teacher generally teaches from the front of the room, the hard-of-hearing child should be seated in the front, preferably slightly off-center toward the windows. This allows the child to hear better and read lips more effectively. Light should be directed toward the teacher's face and away from the speech reader's eyes.

- If the child's hearing impairment involves only one ear, or if the impairment is greater in one ear than the other, the child should be seated in the front corner seat such that his better ear is toward the teacher.

- The teacher should pay attention to the posture of the hearing impaired child's head. The habits of extending the head or twisting the neck to hear better can become firmly fixed.

- The child should be encouraged to watch the face of the teacher whenever he or she is talking to the child. The teacher should speak at the speech reader's eye level whenever possible.

- The teacher should try to face the hard-of-hearing child as much as possible when speaking to the class. An effort should be made to give all important instructions from a position close to the child. It's best not to speak between the child and the windows, which may prove distracting.

- The teacher should not speak loudly or use exaggerated lip movements when speaking to the hard-of-hearing child.

- The hearing impaired child should be encouraged to turn around to watch the faces of children who are reciting.

- It is easy to overestimate the hearing efficiency of a child. It should be remembered that it takes a greater effort for a hearing impaired child to hear than it does for a normal child. It may as a result be more difficult to hold the hearing impaired child's attention.

- A hearing loss of long duration can cause a person's voice to become dull and monotonous. It can also result in poor diction. The hearing impaired child and the rest of the class should be encouraged to speak clearly and distinctly.

- An interest in music and participation in vocal music should be encouraged.

- Since a hearing loss affects all the language processes, the child should be encouraged to compensate by taking a greater interest in reading, grammar, spelling, original writing, and other activities that involve language.

- The hard-of-hearing child should be observed carefully to ensure that he doesn't withdraw or suffer emotionally as a direct or indirect result of his hearing.

- The hard-of-hearing child should participate actively in all plays and other activities which involve speech.

- Teacher should watch carefully for illnesses in hearing impaired children. Colds, influenza, throat and nose infections, tonsilitis, and other ailments should be treated as soon as possible.

- The teacher should be able to assist the child who wears a hearing aid in the classroom.

FIGURE 4-4

these require the cooperation of parents, teachers, and medical doctors. (See Figure 4-5.)

ASSISTING THE CHILD WITH AN ATTENTION DEFICIT IN THE CLASSROOM

Classroom interventions that teachers have found helpful are:

● the use of carrels in the classroom;

● the child listening to soft music through earphones when doing independent work;

● behavior modification techniques, using reinforcers to gradually build a longer attention span;

● shorter assignments with more frequent breaks;

● integrating movement into the teaching of concepts;

● timed tasks such as precision teaching;

● computer aided instruction;

● specific activities designed to enhance their self-esteem.

FIGURE 4-5

STANDARDIZED TESTING

No discussion of assessment can be complete without discussion of standardized testing. During the past decade, the whole process and use of standardized tests has come under a great deal of scrutiny by professional organizations, parent associations, and governments. Often the results of standardized testing have been used negatively. In many cases, the results have merely been used to place a diagnostic label on a child in order to have them placed in special education or as a reason given for lack of success in teaching the child.

In school systems where test results have been used to better understand a child and to plan an appropriate educational program for him, testing does not have the negative connotations that it has in systems where it has been primarily used for labeling.

In his book, *Intelligent Testing with the WISC—R*, Alan Kaufman states that: "The main goal of this book, therefore, is to integrate the theoretical with the practical so as to make the WISC—R a valued tool rather than a feared weapon." (WISC—R is the Wechsler Intelligence Scale for Children—Revised.) Dr. Kaufman and his wife, Nadeen, have recently developed a test, the K-ABC (Kaufman Assessment Battery for Children), which has been designed to take a new look at what we call intelligence, and more importantly, to analyze a child's primary mode of learning as to whether it is sequential or simultaneous. In addition to this, the K-ABC takes into account previous experiences by separating intelligence scores from achievement scores within the same battery of subtests.

Regardless of what instruments are used to measure intelligence, the important aspect is what will be done with the information to best assist the child.

There are many fine references available on standardized testing which discuss the purposes of each test and the validity and reliability statistics. (References included at end of chapter.) These include both group and individual tests used to measure intelligence, perception, academic achievement, and diagnostic tests used to assist in pinpointing specific problems in academic areas. In addition, there are standardized assessment tools to measure general and occupational interests, social and emotional development, and adaptive behavior.

REPORTING TEST RESULTS

Regardless of the instruments used, assessment is the gathering of data about a child and should be utilized to better understand and assist this child. It has long been a complaint of parents and teachers that reports of psychological or psycho-educational testing have done nothing more than give back the same information in confusing words, which they gave when they initially made the referral.

One must keep in mind that assessment in isolation is not the answer but that assessment must lead to appropriate programming. It is sound educational policy that upon completion of a total assessment, parents (and in some cases, the individual assessed) should receive a complete interpretation, and copies of the assessment results.

Schools have an obligation to review with parents assessments done by professionals outside of the school system and to utilize all information in cooperatively planning an appropriate program. Programs should be planned by school personnel and parents together in an attempt to fully utilize all home, school, and community resources.

Following initial assessment and programming, ongoing reevaluation and reassessment should be done to continually ensure that programming is appropriate.

It is therefore extremely important to have reports of standardized tests that are easily understood and that can be utilized for programming. One excellent reference for use with the WISC—R is by Whitworth and Sutton and is entitled *WISC—R Compilation: What to Do Now That You Know the Score*. This book gives an explanation of the purpose of each subtest, factors affecting the subtest, academic performance, and the educational significance of each subtest. In addition to this, the authors point out long-term goals for the learner and list short-term objectives and programs and materials designed to reach these objectives.

Another excellent kit that can be utilized for assisting teachers to understand different learning styles is the "Kaufman Sequential or Simultaneous Workshop Kit." This kit gives examples of significant learning strengths and weaknesses and assists teachers in designing alternative lesson plans. This kit also gives many fine examples to assist parents in understanding their child's learning style.

EDUCATIONAL ASSESSMENT PROFILES

Assessment reports can be equally confusing to teachers unless they make specific recommendations that have direct applicability in the classroom. One of the difficulties in reporting psychological test information is to relate the variety of tests to each other. This has been difficult because of test results being reported in a variety of ways. For example: quotients, grade equivalents, stanines, percentiles, and age equivalents.

The authors wish to include an educational assessment profile that has proven to be extremely useful to them over the past two decades in not only analyzing the wide variety of tests and their scores, but for explaining the test results to both parents and teachers. These profiles are useful for setting priorities and goals when establishing a program to assist the child assessed. In utilizing this profile, a solid line in one color can be drawn across at the child's chronological age level, which is listed on the extreme right hand side of the page. A line in a different color can be drawn across at his current grade level. Once this is accomplished, it brings into perspective the variety of scores that the child received on the psycho-educational test battery. In the small squares across the top, the tests and subtests can be broken down by specific areas and the scores achieved in these tests can be listed in the boxes at the bottom. In addition to these, tests reported in age equivalents can be quickly plotted by following the age scale on the right hand side of the page. Scores listed in grade equivalents can be plotted by following the grade equivalent scale on the far left hand side of the page.

Those scores such as I.Q. must be simply converted to mental age scores by using the I.Q. formula $I.Q. = \dfrac{M.A.}{C.A.} \times 100$

In following this procedure, it is recommended that both chronological age and mental age be converted into months for the greatest degree of accuracy.

A further benefit of the profile sheet is its ability to graphically point out areas of strength and weakness. Although a variety of assessment instruments are used, the common areas of weakness seem to stand out significantly as do the areas of strength. One can quickly observe these areas, whether they are subtest sections of general intelligence tests, perceptual tests, or diagnostic educational tests. This can prove especially helpful in planning an individualized program for the child. More than one set of scores can be plotted on the same profile sheet in order to graphically show a child's progress between assessments. This can be accomplished by using different colors to represent the scores at different testing times.

Figure 4-6 is a sample blank profile sheet which can be reproduced if the reader finds this useful. Figure 4-7 is an example of an actual case where this profile sheet was used for programming showing the student in September (Figure 4-7) and then again in May (Figure 4-8). Progress was charted using the same instruments in reassessment as were used in the initial assessment.

To enable the reader to understand the completed profile sheets, it is necessary to know what test instruments were used.

The first seven blocks on the top going from left to right are from French's Pictorial Test of Intelligence. An explanation of the abbreviations is listed below:

- P.V. — Picture Vocabulary
- F.D. — Form Discrimination
- I & C — Information and Comprehension
- Sim. — Similarities
- S & #C — Size and Number Concept
- I.R. — Immediate Recall
- M.A. — Mental Age

The final six blocks represent scores on the Frostig Developmental Test of Visual Perception. An explanation of the abbreviations is listed below:

- E.M. — Eye Motor Coordination
- F.G. — Figure Ground Discrimination
- F.C. — Form Constancy
- P.S. — Position in Space
- S.R. — Spatial Relations

The solid line across the profile sheet represents the student's chronological age and is derived from the ages listed in years and months on the right column.

The broken (- · -) line across the profile sheet represents the student's grade placement which is derived from the grade levels listed on the left-hand column.

The asterisks on the profile sheets represent the numerical scores listed in the box directly below.

Although the name is fictitious, these profile sheets represent an assessment completed with an actual child.

The first assessment was completed early in the year because of various possible developmental lags observed in the preschool screening. In other

NAME: _____ DATE: _____

GRADE

AGE

	12-3 12-0 11-9
6.0	
	11-3 11-0 10-9
5.0	
	10-3 10-0 9-9
4.0	
	9-3 9-0 8-9
3.0	
	8-3 8-0 7-9
2.0	
	7-3 7-0 6-9
1.0	
	6-3 6-0 5-9
P(K)	
	5-3 5-0 4-9
	4-3 4-0 3-9
	3-3 3-0 2-9

FIGURE 4-6

76

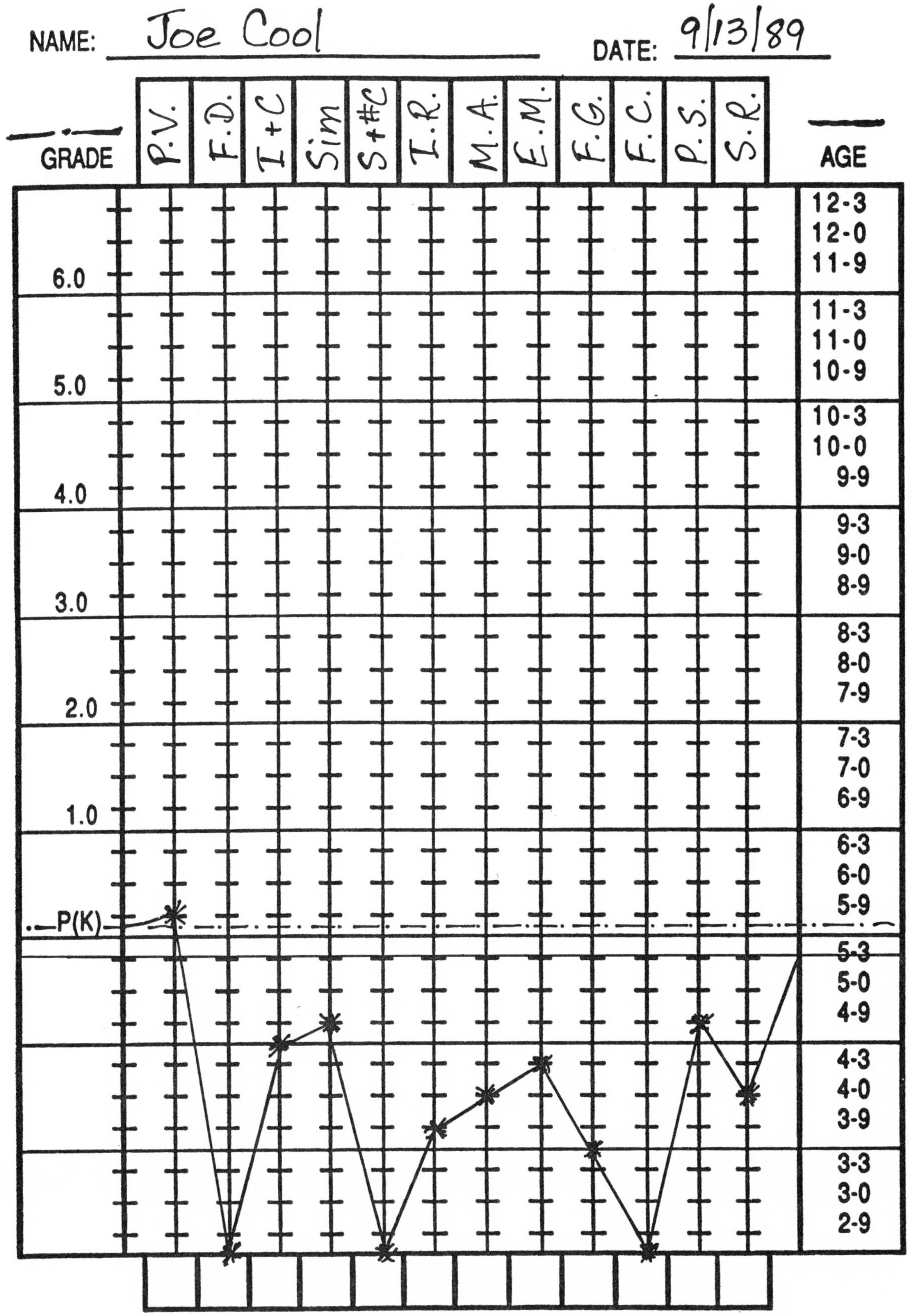
NAME: Joe Cool
DATE: 9/13/89
GRADE
P.V.
F.D.
I+C
Sim
S+#C
I.R.
M.A.
E.M.
F.G.
F.C.
P.S.
S.R.
AGE
6.0
5.0
4.0
3.0
2.0
1.0
P(K)
12-3
12-0
11-9
11-3
11-0
10-9
10-3
10-0
9-9
9-3
9-0
8-9
8-3
8-0
7-9
7-3
7-0
6-9
6-3
6-0
5-9
5-3
5-0
4-9
4-3
4-0
3-9
3-3
3-0
2-9

FIGURE 4-7

NAME: _Joe Cool_   DATE: _5/2/90_

GRADE	P.V.	F.D.	I+C	Sim.	S+#C	I.R.	M.A.	E.M.	F.G.	F.C.	P.S.	S.R.	AGE
													12-3 12-0 11-9
6.0													
													11-3 11-0 10-9
5.0													
													10-3 10-0 9-9
4.0													
													9-3 9-0 8-9
3.0													
													8-3 8-0 7-9
2.0													
													7-3 7-0 6-9
1.0													
													6-3
													6-0
P(K)													5-9
													5-3 5-0 4-9
													4-3 4-0 3-9
													3-3 3-0 2-9

FIGURE 4-8

78

words, this child was a potential high-risk for failure.

The second assessment was completed in May. During the period of time between the two assessments, this student received an individualized program within the regular classroom.

Very quickly, by looking at the two profile sheets, one can readily see the growth that has taken place, as well as the areas still requiring individualized programming.

Although the sample profile sheets are those of a very young child, they can also be used for older children by adjusting the age and grade columns.

The authors purposely selected a young child for this example to demonstrate how assessment and programming can be utilized to prevent failure and frustration in young children.

INTERPRETING THE EDUCATIONAL ASSESSMENT

Ideally the case conference should include the parents, (the child, depending on age), the classroom teacher, the school principal or supervisor, and the resource teacher, as well as the psychologist or psychometrist who conducted the testing. During the case conference, the test results should be treated only as one piece of information about the child. The tone of the case conference must be designed to make the parents feel comfortable and knowledgeable about their own child. It should be approached as a problem-solving session where all of the data gathered on the child is openly discussed. Some general consensus should be reached regarding the best possible placement for the child, as well as general guidelines about his program requirements. In addition to this, it is helpful to discuss who will be responsible for various parts of the child's program and how this may be coordinated.

No discussion of assessment would be complete without mentioning the need for periodic reassessment and ongoing informal assessment. These factors are important to assess not only student achievement, but program effectiveness. There may be need for additional data gathering and referrals both within the system and to outside agencies and professionals in cases where there is lack of progress.

MAKING PLACEMENT DECISIONS

Placement decisions can be difficult for all concerned — parents as well as school personnel. Often there is no ideal placement for a given student. Even if the school has completed an educational assessment, this is only part of the picture. School personnel should explain all of the possible options to parents highlighting what they believe to be the positive and negative features of each option. Professionals have an obligation to recommend to parents what they consider to be the best possible placement for their child at the present time. However, it should be made clear that the final decision concerning placement is that of the parents for the following reasons:

- Parents have the ultimate responsibility for the child.

- Value systems may differ from school personnel, e.g., parents may be more concerned about social integration than academic progress.

- Home and school cooperation is essential. This may not occur if parents feel their desires are disregarded.

- Placement options may be very confusing for parents when discussed at a meeting. Parents should be encouraged to visit and view firsthand the alternative placements discussed.

- Parents should not be pressured for a rapid decision, but should be given time to process the information presented.

- Reassurance must be given to parents that if a placement is not working satisfactorily, a change can be made.

- Time and the possibility of change affords parents an opportunity to work out feelings of frustration or denial.

- Evaluation and ongoing review are essential in maintaining the best possible placement. Parents must be informed if changes in placement are indicated.

- Disruptive behavior that is having a negative effect on the learning of the other children in the classroom may necessitate a change in placement.

In the vast majority of cases, this cooperative type of placement procedure will avoid placements being decided by the legal system rather than by parents and educators. Parents of special-needs children can often receive much needed support from other parents with similar concerns. It may be helpful to suggest to parents how to contact parent groups such as the local autistic society, etc.

PARENT SUPPORT

Often professionals in one field are confused when dealing with professionals from another field. This may be due to the lack of face-to-face discussion, lack of awareness of each other's perceived role, and a lack of understanding of each other's professional jargon.

One can imagine how confusing dealing with a variety of professionals can be for most parents. As educators we have a responsibility to make parents aware of available support services. It is helpful to have information available in order to refer parents to appropriate advocacy organizations. Many of these organizations have information and programs to assist parents and families.

Following are reprints produced for parents by the Canadian Association for Children and Adults with Learning Disabilities and are designed to assist them during their meetings with professionals. (Used with permission of CACLD.)

PARENT/TEACHER INTERVIEWS

This pamphlet is written to assist the parents who have a sincere desire to help their child with special needs. Parents should become as knowledgeable as possible about their child's problems.

The first obligation of the parent is to act as an advocate for the child, a process which will begin anew with each new school year or social setting. It is also assumed that the parent will approach each interview with an open mind and heart, prepared to consider suggestions made by the teacher. Parents must approach the situation with as much objectivity as they can muster, realizing that they are not responsible for their child's problems, but are nevertheless determined to help to the best of their ability. Sometimes parents will have suggestions to help the teacher deal with the child. Sometimes the teacher will have suggestions to help the child in school and at home. Parents will only find out which situation they are in if they approach each interview with an open mind.

With these thoughts in mind, the following steps are suggested for maximum satisfaction from a parent/teacher interview:

1. Listen.
2. Empathize.
3. Question.
4. Ask for suggestions about what parents might do.
5. Respond to suggestions.
6. Share knowledge and experience gained from the past.

Listen

Listen to what the teacher wishes to tell you. Listen to EVERYTHING without offering an opinion of your own at this time. Encourage the teacher to be very specific about his/her concerns for your child. Only if the teacher senses from your silence and encouragement that you are prepared to accept what his/her thoughts, feelings, concerns, or frustrations are, will you truly find out what he/she thinks and feels about your child. There are many good books available on the subject of listening. There are excellent sections in *Teacher Effectiveness Training* by Thomas Gordon which deal with parent/teacher interviews and active listening. This "phase" of listening will help to focus the interview on the greatest immediate need of your child as it relates to this teacher. Try to determine whether achievement or behavior is the major trouble area in this situation.

Empathize

Whatever problem the teacher may be having with your child at school will probably not be news to you. Tell him/her that you understand. Tell him/her you are aware of how difficult/challenging/frustrating/disruptive, etc. your child can be. This will indicate to the teacher that you do not demand or expect him/her to perform miracles, and that you are prepared to accept and deal with the reality of the situation. The teacher may be as unsure as you are about how to help your child, or even of what to say to you.

Question

- Ask any question you have about your child's performance in any specific area. Ask about what, if any, testing has been done to diagnose his problems. Ask to see those test results if you wish, or to have a copy for your records, or to have an appointment with the tester to discuss the results. It is a good idea to come to the interview with specific questions you might have written down. That will ensure that you don't forget to get some information you wanted. (If no testing has been done, you might request it at this time.) Insist on appropriate testing and/or referrals, and on access to information. Your ongoing task of being an advocate for your child will be easier if you have complete records.

- Find out what steps have been taken to help the student, either within the class or outside the classroom, to help solve the problem. Be sure you understand completely what these steps are.

- Explore with the teacher what possible alternatives exist either in the school, the school system, or the community which might provide appropriate placement or services for your child. Some questions to ask:

    1. In what subject area does he/she need special help?
    2. What are his/her strongest skills in school?
    3. How does he/she relate to the other children in the class?
    4. How are his/her study and work habits?

Ask for Teacher's Suggestions

Ask the teacher if there is any way in which you might be able to help your child to achieve to his/her potential.

Respond to Suggestions

At this point it is time for you to bring your child's life style into the child/teacher situation. If the teacher's suggestions are feasible, you can accept them, and work out a suitable system for communication and follow-through. If the suggestions are not feasible, because of your life style, your relationship with your child, your ability to work with your child, your assessment of your child's needs and capabilities, or any other factor, your opinion and the reasons for it must be shared with the teacher. You have a responsibility to ensure that the teacher recognizes the special needs of your child. Make it clear that you intend to be an active partner in the education of your child, and will expect to communicate with the teacher on a regular basis.

Share Knowledge and Past Experiences

It is a good idea to share with the teacher any procedures that have worked well in the past. You are the one who sees your child relate or not relate to teachers and/or situations over many years. You can prevent much trial and error by sharing such information with the teacher. You should also tell the teacher what things or attitudes have a negative effect on your child's behavior and/or achievement. Include pertinent medical diagnosis and treatment.

By this time you and the teacher should be able to design a plan which will offer your child the support and services he needs, and an agreement to communicate regularly.

Should you come away from the interview feeling that the teacher is not prepared to accept your child and deal with his/her special needs, you may wish to pursue alternative placement. This could mean simply a change to another teacher, to a different type of class, or to a different school. Children with special needs have a difficult enough time in school without going through a year with a teacher who thinks he/she is just lazy, unmotivated, has his/her head in the clouds, won't pay attention, or any of the labels we hear so often. The school principal or Special Education Supervisor may be able to guide your search for a better alternative.

PARENT/PEDIATRICIAN INTERVIEW

If you have any concerns about your child's health, development, coordination, perception, attention span, or learning abilities, you should visit your doctor. Explain to your pediatrician or family doctor that you want his (or her) advice with regard to worries you may have about your child's learning problem or whether there is indeed one present.

If your child is attending school, his (or her) teacher may have made some significant observations or may have been the first to recognize a learning problem. A note from the teacher will be helpful to the doctor.

If any deficiency has been found on visual and auditory screening performed by Public Health or School nurses, this should be brought to the doctor's attention.

You may be asked to complete a questionnaire before your doctor examines your child. Tell the doctor what you and others have noticed about your child. Let him know about your problems and your concerns.

After the doctor has examined your child he may recommend special investigations, medical referrals or referrals to other professionals.

The doctor may prescribe medication, especially if your child is hyperactive or has a short attention span. If medication is recommended, ask about the purpose of it and the response to be expected. Inquire about possible side effects and what effect it may have on appetite, sleep, behavior, and learning ability. Ask how long the medicine should be taken and when the prescription will be renewed or reviewed by the doctor. Be sure you understand the doctor's instructions about the frequency, timing, and amount of medication to be taken. You might like to discuss with the doctor whether there is a suitable alternative to taking the medication and what the effect would be if the medicine is not taken as prescribed, or at all.

Discuss with the doctor his recommendations concerning follow-up examinations. Would he like to see you and your child again about the problem your child may have or even if there is not a problem? If so, at what intervals should you return? Will he or she coordinate referrals and supervise the implementation of recommendations that emanate from there?

Ask the doctor if he will be available to confer with your child's teacher, guidance counselor, or school psychologist. The doctor will want your authorization in writing to permit him to report to or discuss with school authorities his findings and recommendations.

Because oral reports are often lost or confused in the telling, request that he give you a written report which you can then give to the school.

GUIDELINES FOR PARENTS WHEN MEETING WITH PSYCHOLOGISTS

This article is designed to assist you, the parent of a child with special needs, to receive the most benefit from an interview with a psychologist. The writer assumes that the parent reading this has a sincere desire to help the child in any way possible. The writer also assumes that this is not the only publication that you, the parent, have read concerning your child's problems. However, if it is, you should become as knowledgeable as possible.

As a parent, you must realize that the main objective of a psychological assessment is to be able to offer suggestions to you and to school personnel as to the most effective ways of assisting your child. This is true whether the psychologist is employed by the schools, a community agency, or is in private practice. With these thoughts in mind, the following steps are suggested to achieve maximum satisfaction from a Parent Psychologist Interview.

1. Listen carefully and take notes.
2. Question and answer questions.
3. Ask for suggestions about what a parent might do.
4. Respond to these suggestions.
5. Ask for suggestions about what might be done in the school situation.
6. Share knowledge and experience gained from the past.
7. Request a written report.

Listen

Listen carefully before offering an opinion but be sure to ask questions about terms you do not understand. Ask for concrete examples to clarify in your own mind what is being discussed. Encourage the psychologist to go into detail about specific tests or parts of tests that were given to your child and ask how these relate to school work and/or behavior.

Question

Ask questions concerning the tests given and individual parts of the tests, if this is not volunteered in the original explanation. (This is particularly important with most I.Q. tests.) Ask questions not only regarding the weakness that your child has shown in the testing situation but also regarding your child's strengths, as these are equally important to know about. Do not be afraid to question the psychologist about the validity and reliability of the tests given or the testing situation. This is important if the test results do not confirm your own observations or those of your child's teacher(s). It is also appropriate to question the psychologist as to whether or not he/she thinks additional testing or referrals should be made on the basis of their testings. It is also wise to question the psychologist about your child's behavior and willingness to cooperate during the testing situation in order to determine whether or not he/she feels that this had an effect on the test results. If at the time of testing your child was not feeling well or was unusually upset about something, this should be shared with the psychologist.

Parent Suggestions

Ask the psychologist for suggestions on what you, as a parent, might do to assist your child in the areas that were weak in the testing. Also ask for suggestions on how you might utilize your child's strengths in either assisting him/her with his/her learning or helping improve his/her self-concept.

Respond

Respond to suggestions made by the psychologist. This is important as it will allow the psychologist to clarify more specifically what he/she is talking to you about. Also you will be able to let him/her know whether you have tried these things or similar things in the past. Thus when your meeting is completed, you will have some very clear-cut definitive actions that you as a parent might take. Be realistic. Consider honestly how much time you can spend with your child and how well he will do things for you. Discuss this with the psychologist and ask for guidance in choosing the most important skills with which you may assist your child. Discuss with the psychologist your ideas of the other individuals in your child's world who might be better able to assist him/her than you.

School Suggestions

Ask the psychologist for suggestions for the school. Assuming the psychologist with whom you are having the interview is not an employee of the school board, but is a consultant or a private practitioner, you might ask him for suggestions. For instance: How might the school better assist your child in his/her weak areas? Does the psychologist plan to present this information to your child's teacher, principal, or other school personnel? In what form will this information be presented? Such knowledge will prepare you to contact your child's school and will enable you to meet with the principal and the teacher as an informed parent. If the psychologist with whom you are meeting is an employee of the school board, he/she should be able to give you specific information about how the school plans to assist your child.

Knowledge

During the interview with the psychologist, it is important to share information. When suggestions are made for the future, you will probably be reminded of previous experiences. This is an excellent opportunity to share additional information regarding your child's learning and behavior. These past experiences are important for the future. For instance: What things appeared not to have worked at all? What things appeared to work best for your child? It would be helpful also to agree on specific things that the psychologist will recommend to the teacher or to other school personnel. It would also be helpful to establish a schedule; when to visit the school following the interview with the psychologist and the appropriate time to elapse before revisiting the school.

At the conclusion of your interview with the psychologist, it is important to establish the time for another meeting in order to evaluate how well the suggestions for your child's program and activity have been working.

In summary, after meeting with the psychologist who tested your child, you should have the following information:

1. Your child's level of general abilities.

2. Strong and weak areas of intelligence and how this effects his/her school learning or performance.

3. Your child's functional skills including:

   a. Motor functioning

   b. Auditory functioning

   c. Visual functioning

   d. Thinking skills when words are involved

   e. Thinking skills when words are not involved

4. Your child's ability to function in core academic areas of reading, writing, and mathematics, with approximate grade equivalent scores in each.

5. Concrete suggestions for a prescriptive remedial or developmental program for both home and school.

PARENTS AS PARTNERS IN THE
SPECIAL EDUCATIONAL PROGRAMS OF THEIR CHILDREN

Recent Special Education legislation and policy in Canada and the United States have entrenched the right of parents to participate in every decision related to the education of their children with special needs. By including the parents as partners in decision-making, enlightened legislators and professionals are affirming the importance of the participation of parents in this area.

In 1970 the CELDIC Report stressed that the fundamental need for continuity of concern and care for each child with special needs is a reciprocal process requiring an open sharing of information between parents and professionals. It also involves the recognition of the parents' "right to know" and to participate as follows:

- the right to know when psychological assessments, or special evaluations, are considered necessary, and the right therefore to give informed consent;

- the right to know, and to receive a clear explanation of, the results of the testing from the appropriate professional;

- the right to know what educational options in programs and placement are available, and how suitable these options are to the approaches and needs identified by the assessment and by the observations of both teachers and parents;

- the right to consultation on and consent to the Special Education plans for their children, and/or to any changes in those plans;

- the right to meet with teachers, the principal, and others involved, to learn about the program and the instructional objectives; and furthermore, the right to be able to meet with the teachers on a regular basis to discuss their children's progress;

- the right to have access to all records concerning their children.

This process involves the sharing of other relevant information by the parents with the school when that information might have some bearing on school performance. Depending on the situation this would probably include pertinent medical data such as hearing and vision tests, medications, etc. It might also include information on early development, social aptitude, and out-of-school activities, etc.

When parents are included as partners in the special education of their children, a number of positive and essential changes can occur; for instance:

- parents are less likely to reject or distrust the Special Education Program because of inadequate or faulty information;

- parents gain knowledge of their children's learning abilities and disabilities;

- teachers and others involved gain important insight into children based on the long-term experience and knowledge of the parents;

- in an atmosphere of cooperation there is less possibility for teachers and parents to waste valuable time and energy in confrontation and in placing blame;

- parents and teachers are able to proceed amicably and cooperatively with the real task of finding the best possible ways to assist the children to learn and to grow.

CHAPTER 4 REFERENCE MATERIALS

Anastasi, A., *Psychological Testing*, 4th ed., Macmillan Publishing Co., New York, 1976.

Address: Macmillan Publishing Co.
                866 Third Avenue
                New York, NY 10022

Beswick, Joan (ed.), *The Hearing Impaired Child In Public School: A Guide for Administrators and Teachers*, Atlantic Provinces Resource Center for the Hearing Handicapped, Amherst, Nova Scotia, 1985.

Address: Atlantic Provinces Resource Center
                for the Hearing Handicapped
                Amherst, Nova Scotia B4H 3Z6

Blackhurst, A. Edward, and Berdine, William H., *An Introduction to Special Education*, Little, Brown and Co., Boston, MA, 1981.

Address: Little, Brown & Co.
                34 Beacon St.
                Boston, MA 02106

Buros, Oscar (ed.), *The Eighth Mental Measurements Yearbook*, Gryphon Press, Highland Park, NJ, 1978.

Cantwell, D.P., *The Hyperactive Child*, Spectrum Publications, Inc., Englewood Cliffs, NJ, 1975.

Address: Prentice-Hall, Inc.
                Englewood Cliffs, NJ 07632

C.A.C.L.D., *The Parent As Advocate*

Address: C.A.C.L.D
                323 Chapel St., Ottawa
                Ottawa, Ontario K1N 722

Connors, C.K., *Food Additives and Hyperactive Children*, Plenum Press, New York, 1981.

Address: Plenum Publishing Corp.
                233 Spring St.
                New York, NY 10013

Elks Purple Cross Deaf Detection and Development Program

Address: 3420A Hill Ave.
             Regina, Saskatchewan
             S4S OW9

Feingold, Benjamin, *Why Your Child Is Hyperactive*, Random House, New York, 1974.

Feingold, Helene, and Feingold, Benjamin, *The Feingold Cookbook for Hyperactive Children and Others with Problems Associated with Food Additives and Salicylates*, Random House, New York, 1979.

Address: Random House, Inc.
             201 E. 50th St.
             New York, NY 10022

Kaufman, Alan S., *Intelligent Testing with the WISC-R*, John Wiley & Sons, New York, 1979.

Address: John Wiley & Sons
             605 Third Avenue
             New York, NY 10158

Kaufman, Alan, and Kaufman, Nadeen, *Kaufman Assessment Battery for Children*, American Guidance Services, Inc., Circle Pines, MN, 1983.

Kaufman, Alan; Kaufman, Nadeen; and Goldsmith, Bonnie, *Kaufman Sequential or Simultaneous*, American Guidance Services, Inc., Circle Pines, MN, 1984.

Address: American Guidance Services, Inc.
             Circle Pines, MN 55014-1796

Kinsbourne, M., and Caplan, P.J., *Children's Learning and Attention Problems*, Little, Brown & Co., Boston, 1979.

Address: Little, Brown & Co.
             34 Beacon St.
             Boston, MA 02106

Macmillan, D.L., *Behavior Modification in Education*, Macmillan Publishing Co., New York, 1973.

Address: Macmillan Publishing Co.
             866 Third Avenue
             New York, NY 10022

Optometric Extension Program Foundation, Inc. *Educators Guide to Classroom Vision Problems*, Duncan, OK, 1968.

Address: Optometric Extension Program Foundation
             Section on Children's Vision Care & Guidance
             Duncan, OK 73533

Ross, D.M. and Ross, S.A., *Hyperactivity — Research, Theory, Action*, John Wiley & Sons, New York, 1976.

Address: John Wiley & Sons
             605 Third Avenue
             New York, NY 10158

Simpson, D.D., and Nelson, A.E. "Breathing Control and Attention Training," U.S. Educational Resources Information Center, *ERIC Document*, ED063723, 1977.

Address: EPIC Document Reproduction Service
              3900 Wheeler Ave.
              Alexandria, VA 22304

Swanson, H.L., and Watson, B.L., *Educational; and Psychological Assessment of Exceptional Children: Theories, Strategies and Applications*, C.V. Mosby Co., St. Louis, MO, 1982.

Address: 11830 West Industrial Drive
              St. Louis, MO 63146

Thorndike, R.L., and Hagen, E., *Measurement and Evaluation in Psychology and Education*, 4th ed., John Wiley & Sons, New York, 1977.

Address: John Wiley & Sons
              605 Third Avenue
              New York, NY 10158

White, Burton, "The Critical Importance of Hearing Ability," *The Center for Parent Education Newsletter*, Vol. 1; Nos. 3 and 4, Newton, MA, 1979.

Address: The Center for Parent Education
              55 Chapel St.
              Newton, MA 02160

Whitworth, John, and Sutton, Dorothy, *WISC-R Compilation: What to Do Now That You Know the Score*, Academic Therapy Publications, Novato, CA, 1978.

Address: Academic Therapy Publications
              20 Commercial Boulevard
              Novato, CA 94947

Ysseldyke, James E., and Salvia, John, *Assessment in Special Remedial Education* (2nd ed.), Houghton Mifflin Co., Boston, 1981.

Address: Houghton Mifflin Co.
              One Beacon St.
              Boston, MA 02108

CHAPTER 5

The Roles of
the Resource Teacher

*We consider the child's social awareness and adaptability
to be the most critical factor . . . a better predictor of his
future adjustment than the grades he obtains.*

Marianne Frostig

The resource teacher, to be effective, must be perceived as the person in the school who can serve as a resource to the principal, teachers, parents, and children. Over time the role of resource teacher has evolved from remedial tutor to the person in the school who has a variety of skills to offer to the school and community in general. Ideally, the resource teacher should be an individual who possesses flexibility and creativity in approaching educational problems. The resource teacher who works at both the elementary school and secondary school levels must use different strategies and methods in these two situations when working with students and staff. This is due to vast differences in organization and expectations at different levels of education.

In addition to awareness of the school, the resource teacher must be aware of strengths and weaknesses within the community. The primary role of the resource teacher is to assist children having learning difficulties to improve their self-esteem. Resource teachers therefore must be aware of the five essential elements of self-esteem:

- sense of security;
- sense of identity;
- feeling of belonging;
- sense of purpose;
- sense of personal competence.

In order to accomplish improved self-esteem with students having learning difficulties, the resource teacher must be willing and able to use a variety of approaches and strategies, not only when dealing with the child, but also when dealing with the significant others in the child's world. The five primary roles of the resource teacher are:

- assessment and programming with shared responsibility;
- consultative role with the classroom teacher;
- utilizing community resources;
- acting as liaison with and reporting to parents;
- establishing volunteer programs.

ASSESSMENT AND PROGRAMMING

During the past two decades, these roles have remained consistent. However the emphasis placed on each has changed greatly. Resource teachers' roles in assessment and consultation have continually increased, while the role in direct instruction has gradually decreased over this time period. This has made the resource teacher a more effective resource, not only to the child, but to the school staff and parents.

The resource teacher must be the person responsible for coordinating assessment and developing programs for each child referred. It is ideal if the resource teacher has the certification and the skills to be able to do all of the standardized tests required in the assessment. However, in many cases, they may require the assistance of someone else in the system to administer the restricted tests. The resource teacher is the one individual who has the best opportunity to discuss the child with his current teacher, past teachers, and parents, as well as to make direct observation within the classroom. Because the resource teacher is a member of the school staff, she/he has an excellent opportunity to make suggestions to teachers and parents when problems first arise and to monitor progress prior to a formal referral being submitted.

SHARED RESPONSIBILITY

In detailing the individualized program for children having learning difficulties within the school system, the authors believe that certain guidelines should be followed. The basic principle of this is "shared responsibility." For example, the classroom teacher, the Special Education teacher, and the parents, should work as a team in the education of an individual child.

It is essential to look at the total child, not just academic needs. Social and emotional needs must be viewed as being as important as academic needs when a program is being planned. It is suggested that at least three segments be devised for each individualized program and often more than that are required. The three basic components are:

- a home program basically designed with those activities that are game-like and fun in nature;
- a classroom program that attempts to teach the child through the areas of strengths and assists when compensating for the areas of weaknesses;
- a tutorial program where a child can work on the areas of weakness in a more secure, less embarrassing, small group situation.

The authors have discovered over the years that there are several advantages of using shared responsibility and team work:

- Positive lines of communication are developed between Special Education staff and the parents.
- Positive lines of communication are developed between Special Education staff and classroom teachers.
- This approach eliminates much frustration felt by parents of a handicapped child. So often they simply need to know what to do.
- When mainstreaming Special Education students into regular classrooms, it is important for the child's growth to have a program developed for the regular classroom teacher.

It must be remembered that this approach is not to be compared to I.E.P.s. This is not a contract, rather a guide with which to operate. For example, not all parents are comfortable working with their own children, just as not all teachers are comfortable working with learning disabled children. Flexibility and adaptability are critical factors when using this approach.

Programs for the regular classroom can be modified as the need arises, usually a check at the beginning of every month will be sufficient.

When the parents complete activities given to them, more difficult developmental tasks can be provided by the resource teacher. The home program can be more flexible, giving the parents the freedom to contact the school as needed.

In addition to this, it is very often helpful to determine if there are existing programs in the community which would be of assistance to the child and his/her family. It may be that in rural areas, some obviously helpful programs in the community do not exist, but with parents and professionals working together often these programs can be established.

When groups of parents in a particular school or area need assistance in working with their child, the professional staff of the school can assist them by running short courses and by monitoring discussion groups to assist parents. One example of this is the Hanen Early Language Program, which comes complete with video tapes and textbooks for parents, giving them many hints and clues in assisting their children with their language development.

SAVING TIME IN PROGRAMMING

Writing individual programs is difficult and tedious work, and more often than not, resource teachers rewrite the same or similar information over and over again during the course of a year. Several years ago, the authors, along with several colleagues, attempted to alleviate this problem by taking on the major task of synthesizing initial programs from a variety of developmental age-sequenced commercial programs on the market. Major areas of perceptual functioning were divided with the following guidelines, to develop for each important area of perceptual functioning a combination of three programs at each developmental age. Starting with developmental age four years, zero months, one program was to be game-like activities that could be done at home in a "fun" setting. The second program was one that could be carried out in a regular classroom with the full knowledge that there will be 25 to 30 additional students in that classroom. The third program was one that could be carried out by a tutor with a small group of children giving more assistance with some tasks.

When these activities are mastered by the child, the individuals involved receive additional activities at a developmental age norm approximately six months more advanced. The areas covered are auditory memory and sequencing, auditory discrimination, visual memory, visual discrimination, visual motor integration, gross motor coordination, agility, and a variety of other perceptual tasks.

Once this major project was accomplished, resource teachers were able to organize these materials in their file and have them at their fingertips when putting together an individualized program for any student with developmental lags up to age ten. Both parents and classroom teachers were extremely pleased with the speed at which they received concrete activities to help a child following the initial case conference.

Since most children have more than one area which needed this type of programming, a good deal of variety of was built into the program.

Figures 5-1, 5-2, and 5-3 are examples of this programming utilizing home, classroom teacher, and tutor. Listed at the beginning of each program is the perceptual area to be remediated, the approximate developmental age, and the place where these activities are to be conducted. The example given is taken from a variety of commercial programs which are listed in the references at the end of this chapter.

CONSULTATIVE ROLE WITH CLASSROOM TEACHERS

The classroom teacher and resource teacher should discuss how they might organize the classroom to give special instruction to a variety of students in

VISUAL MOTOR INTEGRATION (5-0) — CLASSROOM

1. <u>Hold your head still.</u>

Have the children sit in front of you. Ask the children to follow an object with their eyes without moving their heads. Move the object slowly from left to right at the children's eye level. Then, move the object up and down diagonally until it disappears from their vision. Make sure each child's eyes follow the object.

2. <u>Line up.</u>

Line up objects or pictures and have the children count or name them from left to right.

3. <u>Mazes.</u>

Give the children mazes to work with. Find or make mazes that show a left-to-right progression.

4. <u>Pouring.</u>

● Pour into a big bowl.

Have the children pour from a one-half-cup spouted measuring cup into a nine-inch bowl from six inches above the bowl.

● Pour into a small bowl.

Have the children pour from a one-cup spouted measuring cup into a six-inch bowl from twelve inches above the bowl.

● Pour into a big cup.

Have the children pour from a one-pint pitcher into coffee cups placed around a table.

● Pour into a small cup.

Have the children pour from a one-pint pitcher into small six-ounce paper cups placed around a table.

● The child will demonstrate the ability to pour accurately. Using a spouted measuring cup filled to the one-half-cup line with rice, the child will pour the rice into a coffee cup. Demonstrate the activity for the child first.

5. <u>Dress the doll.</u>

Give the children dolls to dress and undress. The doll clothing should have snaps, buttons, hooks, zippers, and laces for the children to work with.

6. <u>Corner Practice.</u>

Provide children with an 8½" x 11" paper on which an 8" x 8" square is drawn. Have them cut along the line. Give them another piece of paper with a triangle drawn on it measuring eight inches along the base. After cutting out the shapes they can put them together to form a house.

7. Cut out the shapes.

Have the children cut out geometric forms such as: circles, squares, rectangles, triangles, etc. Save the shapes for the next activity.

8. Paste the shapes.

Give the children a piece of paper that has the outlines of the shapes they cut from the activity above. Tell the children to paste each cutout shape on the outline that matches it.

9. Art Project.

Have the class cut out geometric shapes to make "modern art" pictures — use different color construction paper.

● cutting corners

Have the children cut the corners of paper into curves.

● ghosts

Have the children cut outlined ghosts.

● ink blots

Have the children cut out ink or paint blot designs.

Choral reading with finger plays that encourage the development of finger dexterity.

Trace own hands.

10. Follow the ball.

Have the children sit on the floor. Stand in front of the children. Move a ball from the children's left to their right. Tell the children to follow the ball with their eyes without moving their heads. Make sure each child can follow the object without turning the head.

11. Old clothes.

Old clothes with buttons, snaps, belts, hooks, zippers, and laces may be used for the children to practice on.

12. Rabbit ears bow.

Show the children how to make a rabbit ears bow with a shoelace after they have laced their shoes. Make the initial tie for the children. Then have them make a loop with one end of the lace in the other hand. Demonstrate how to tie the two rabbit ears together. Give the children long shoelaces to work with. They should have six to eight inches on each end of the lace to make a rabbit ears bow.

The child is to button and zip fasteners as described below:

Button three 3/4-inch buttons into one-inch button holes.

Zip and unzip a jacket while wearing it. Start the zipper for the child.

The child will button two of the three buttons on a garment while wearing it and will zip and unzip a jacket.

Let them practice continually getting themselves ready to go out.

13. Color large letters and numbers.

Coloring activities using simple shapes and one color. Start to teach primary colors.

FIGURE 5-1

VISUAL MOTOR INTEGRATION (5-0) — TUTOR

● Teach the child how to color with proper arm and hand movements, teach circular movements, making sure he/she is holding the crayon properly. Have child spread his/her fingers out on the table; start slowly and have the child poke the space between his/her fingers with the index finger of the dominant hand, other hand.

Speed us as he/she progresses, have him/her keep time with a metronome or music.

● Use picture lacing cards.

● Use large pegboard, patterns using more than four pegs. Make sure the child is comfortable with this before moving on to small pegboards. Child will duplicate pattern — use more than four pegs.

● The child will draw two recognizable 5" squares in imitation with four relatively square corners connected to four relatively straight lines.

MATERIALS: portable blackboard, chalk, plain unlined paper (several sheets), large diameter pencils or crayons, one large and one small square tracing pattern.

TECHNIQUE: Demonstrate drawing a square to the child on the blackboard or on the portable slate. Instruct the child to draw the same. Guide his/her hand if necessary. Instruct the child to trace over the square which you have previously drawn. Erase and have the child draw several more squares. Use the large pattern and have the child trace around the square. Assist by holding the pattern in place and guiding his/her hand. Carry over this activity at the table with paper and pencil or crayon. Discuss things that are square that you can see in the room. Have the child trace the small pattern and then draw several squares free hand. Give assistance when necessary and always praise success.

MEASUREMENT: The child will draw two recognizable squares in imitation on cue of adult, four out of five trials.

- The child is able to color a circle staying within a circle 80% of the time.

  MATERIALS: crayons, paper, cardboard with circle cut out of it (template).

  TECHNIQUE: 1. Place cardboard template on piece of paper instructing child to color entire circle with crayon.
                  2. When he/she can fill in the circle completely, give him/her a sheet of paper with same sized circle drawn. Have entire background on outside of circle colored in. Using a contrasting colored crayon, have child color in circle.
                  3. Next, give child sheet of paper with darkly outlined circle. Follow same procedure.

  MEASUREMENT: The child will be able to color within a circle 8 out of 10 trials, keeping coloring strokes within the line. Note: do not worry if circle is not completely filled in with color.

- The child can place ten dried beans in the mouth of a pop bottle within 20 seconds three of five trials.

  MATERIALS: pop bottle, ten dried beans or small buttons.

  TECHNIQUE: Demonstrate to the child placing beans in bottle. Have child repeat. If the child has difficulty, practice should begin with containers with larger openings.

  Variation: Pick up beans with tweezers and then drop into the bottle.

  MEASUREMENT: Success attained when child deposits ten dried beans into empty pop bottle three out of five trials.

- Makes clay shapes put together with two to three parts.

  WHAT TO DO:
  1. You and child each roll five clay balls. Show child how to stick balls together to form a body of a gingerbread man, a snowman, a rabbit, a cat, etc. Tell him/her to copy your model. Verbally cue him/her on placing the parts.
  2. You and child each roll five "sticks" plus a rectangle. Show child how you attach "sticks" to form legs and tail for an animal or legs for a chair, table, etc. Let clay dry and use objects as play furniture for the animal shapes made of clay.
  3. Practice using bread or cookie dough to make man and animals. Reinforce the child by letting him/her eat the finished product.
  4. Use marshmallows and have the child stick them together with frosting to practice making shapes.
  5. Use sand and water mixture to make shapes.

- The child will follow vertical, horizontal, circular, and diagonal movements with both eyes together with smooth uninterrupted eye movements 100% of the time.

MATERIALS:	Pencil with eraser. Small appropriate holiday cut-out shape, such as heart, Christmas tree, etc., about one inch high. This cut-out should be tacked to the eraser of the pencil.
TECHNIQUE:	Teacher holds the pencil approximately 14" from the child's eyes. Tell the child he/she should keep his/her head still and move only his/her eyes to follow the heart, Christmas tree, etc., as it moves. Move the pencil horizontally in both directions, then up and down, then diagonally in both directions, then in a circular motion. The child should not move his/her head, and his/her eye movements should be smooth and uninterrupted. Be sure the child is watching the moving target and not watching the teacher. If the child has great difficulty with these activities after several trials, it might be wise to take him/her to an ophthalmologist for an eye exam.
MEASUREMENT:	The child will follow vertical, horizontal, circular, and diagonal movements with both eyes together with smooth uninterrupted eye movements three out of three trials.

FIGURE 5-2

VISUAL MOTOR INTEGRATION (5-0) — HOME PROGRAM

1. Finger wrestling with Dad - start with thumb and index finger, move on until he/she can comfortably use thumb and little finger.
2. The "Pick up Sticks" game.
3. Large jacks are great, but if this is too difficult you may wish to try this activity at a later time.

Trace the child's hands in sand, or in window fog. Next use crayons, pencils, on plain paper.

4. Let the child play with Mom's mixing bowls, jars, and measuring cups. Water play is a fun addition to this activity.
5. Let the child pour rice, dried beans, etc. from one container to another.
6. Dressing and undressing dolls is good for boys too. You may, however, wish to use super heroes or a favorite dress up doll.
7. A doll that has all kinds of buttons, bows, and zippers to teach the child to button and unbutton, zip and unzip, tie and untie, etc.

99

8. Coloring books with large, simple and well drawn shapes.

9. Dot to dot activities for young children — follow numbers; approximately nine or ten at the beginning.

10. Encourage the child to think of a certain shape; for example, a circle. Now have the child draw any object that he/she thinks of when he/she thinks of that shape. It is fun to have the child color the picture as well.

11. Modeling compound and clay let the child be creative and make whatever shapes he/she wants. Teach him/her how to fill up the molds (if these are available) with the modeling compound or clay. Cookie cutters are also great.

12. Make models of Mom and Dad, pets, friends, cars, houses, etc. Remember to have fun and enjoy playing with the child.

FIGURE 5-3

Figures 5-4 through 5-12 are observational guidelines used to assist teachers in discovering a child's preferred learning style. Also included are suggestions for teaching by way of the child's learning strengths and ideas for remediation of weaknesses.

HOW TO SPOT THE VISUAL LEARNER IN THE CLASSROOM

- Likes to look at books and pictures.
- Loves to look at orderly things — demands neat surroundings.
- Can find what others have lost, remembers where they have seen things.
- Sees details — how you dress, if the slip is showing, errors on typing, etc.
- Can find page in book or workbook readily — may have it half-done before others start.
- Can't get directions orally (if the child is timid, will copy from others rather than ask for more directions). Does better if shown.
- Likes to work puzzles.
- Probably will be able to make good pictures — at least ones with good balance.
- Can set the table correctly, etc.
- May have speech problem.
- May watch teacher's face intently.
- Rarely talks in class — or responds in as few words as possible.
- Hyperactive.

FIGURE 5-4

HOW TO MAKE ADJUSTMENTS FOR THE CHILD

WITH VISUAL MODALITY WEAKNESS IN THE CLASSROOM

- Take out visual distractions. It is impossible to take visuals out of the regular classroom but try to place the child where he is not bombarded by too many visual items. (He/she just swims visually in an overloaded situation.)

- Leave a frame of blank wall around visual displays.

- On worksheets put a heavy line around items to help pupil to attend to one item at a time. (This can often be done to existing ditto sheets. This does not prevent the use of the worksheet with other children.)

- Give him/her a BIG marker.

- Allow him/her to point if necessary. Let him/her touch the first letter of every word.

- Have him/her clear the table top (desk top).

- Let the child get one worksheet at a time from stacks rather than hand the child several papers at once. Also, give the child a purpose for moving about a bit as he/she turns in the completed paper and picks up his/her next sheet from the next stack.

- Try not to stand in front of too cluttered background when instructing him/her. (For some children, it may be necessary for the teacher to wear more simple clothing.)

- Give one step at a time.

FIGURE 5-5

HOW TO TEACH THE CHILD WITH A
STRONG VISUAL MODALITY IN THE CLASSROOM

- Give demonstrations and visual directions in picture, rebus, or written form for tasks.

- Use matching games with concrete objects, illustrations, written symbols.

- Use puzzles of many types for teaching and reinforcing skills.

- Use charts, graphs, maps, filmstrips, and many other visual aids to convey information.

- Use color coding system to teach a sound symbol relationship.

- Draw lines around the configuration of printed words and structural work elements.

- Have children search for letters and words (of which you have shown them a sample) in the printed context of books, magazines, newspapers.

- Have children imitate your tongue and lip placement to reproduce phonetic sounds while looking in a mirror.

- Teach the meaning of diacritical markings as a means of decoding.

- Print the rules for dividing and accenting syllables for children to use as a reference; memorize.

- Encourage the use of the dictionary for word pronunciation clues and language development.

- Provide visual samples and words with directional arrows or color coding for children to trace and copy.

- Provide lined or graph paper for writing.

- Teach math skills with number strips, dominoes, color coded manipulative rulers and protractors, number lines.

Specific Teaching Suggestions

Spelling

1. Spelling words should be chosen from the child's reading vocabulary.

2. First develop an awareness for the number of syllables within words (e.g., say a word, and have the child tap out the rhythm of the syllables).

3. Give a word in syllables and have the child blend the syllables into words (e.g., "mar-ble" is marble). Do this after the child can differentiate the number of syllables in a word.

4. Have the child combine individual sounds into words (e.g., s-t-o-p is stop). The use of cut-out letters for this exercise can provide visual cues.

5. Teach word families, utilizing visual symbols to improve auditory discrimination. Example: late-date-fate-hate.

   a. Underline the parts of the words that are the same.
   b. Say the words to hear the similarity.
   c. Leave out letters and have the child write the word: "I was l... for school." (late)

6. "Listen carefully to the words and write the missing parts." This exercise improves syllabication and spelling.

   Example: mul--ply (multiply) ---pet (carpet)

7. Spelling words should be dictated slowly.

● <u>Written Language — Deficient Formulation and Syntax</u>

1. An important point to consider is the basic principle of recognition before recall. The child should not be required to write until he can identify errors in sentences already written.

2. Write sentences containing a few errors. Read the sentences as they should be and ask the child to tell whether the sentence he hears is the same as the one he/she sees.

   Example:

   Written: Tomorrow we sailing on the lake.

   Read: Tomorrow we will go sailing on the lake.

3. Write sentences as those above but with words transposed for children who make errors of word order.

4. Have child arrange word cards according to a spoken sentence. (Example: "The baseball player hit a home run.") The child places the cards in the proper order, then reads the sentence and writes it, checking his/her work by looking at the arrangement of the cards.

5. Have child self-monitor his/her work by reading it aloud slowly, checking word by word that he/she says exactly what has been written.

6. Have the child give an oral sentence. The teacher writes what he/she says, but omits a word or changes the sentence in some way. The child is asked to find the error in the written sentence.

7. Choose action pictures and write sentences to accompany each one. Write one sentence correctly and others with errors.

   Assume the picture shows a group of children playing football; sentences such as these are written:

   The children is playing football.

   The children are playing football.

   The children are played football.

8. Separate words printed on movable, cardboard strips afford a good way to practice sentence building and other language skills.

   a. Compound words. Combine strips to make compound words.
   cat   fish   hand   shake   grand   father   after   noon

   b. Sentences
   Who   What   Where   When

   The alligator swam in the pond yesterday.

   c. Stories: Arrange the scrambled sentence to make a story.

(1)　　puppy　　has　　a　　Don　　new

(Don has a new puppy.)

(2)　　its　　Rags　　name　　is

(its name is Rags.) etc.

9. Have the child write sentences and listen to the teacher read them aloud to identify the errors auditorily. Corrections are then made on the paper.

● Written Language — Ideation and Productivity

1. As a general principle, training should begin with an oral discussion of experiences and ideas. It is important to follow the progression of experience from auditory language to written language. A second progression is to assist the children in going from concrete to abstract thinking. As another general principle, it is preferable to structure the writing assignment for best results.

2. Concrete-Descriptive (writing about things in a descriptive manner).

   a. Write names of objects: "Ball" — expand this by adding adjectives: "A purple ball," etc.

   b. Use action pictures — "Write a sentence about each picture. In each sentence tell what the person is doing or tell where the person is going." Example: "John is running. John is running to the store. Record oral sentences and write them (sentences about pictures).

3. Concrete-Imaginative (inferring ideas from stimulus picture).

   a. Lead questions help stimulate the imagination: Who is in the picture? What is happening? How did it happen?

4. Abstract-Descriptive (stress on concepts of time, space, and sequence).

   a. Write sentences about individual pictures that tell a story in sequence (e.g., film strips, cartoons).

   b. Keep a diary — write a summary of the week's events in correct sequence.

5. Abstract — imaginative (stories have a plot, setting, figures of speech, continuity).

   a. Exercises such as this facilitate more colorful writing:

   The grass grows as quickly as a _____ .

   The man is as strong as an _____ .

   Choices: ox, elephant, whisker.

   b. Outlining can be taught to aid the development of "story plots." The story could be taped and then written from dictation.

FIGURE 5-6

HOW TO SPOT THE AUDITORY LEARNER IN THE CLASSROOM

- Never shuts up — the chatterer.
- Tells jokes.
- Tries to be funny.
- Can win spelling bees if taught say-spell-say method.
- Good story teller. Stories get taller and taller. Child may have to learn when to stop.
- Hyperactive.
- Poor handwriting — history of reversals.
- If child can make telephone call asking for information you have directed and remember the received message and relay that message back — good sign of auditory strength.
- Likes records, folk dances, rhythmic activities (Note: give the drums, etc. to the auditory learner).
- Probably has ten excuses for everything.
- Knows all the words to all the songs — can memorize easily.
- Motorically awkward.
- Poor performance on group tests of intelligence.
- Seems brighter than group test results indicate.
- Poor perception of time, space.

FIGURE 5-7

**HOW TO MAKE ADJUSTMENT FOR THE CHILD
WITH AUDITORY MODALITY WEAKNESS IN THE CLASSROOM**

- Take out as much noise as possible.
- Find him a quiet place to work.
- Very soft music background may be used but not bouncy music.
- Use as few words as you can.
- If you repeat, use the same words.
- Speak directly to this child.

- Earphones and tape recorder help cut out distraction of other noises.
- Cup your hand about his ear to help him focus on instruction.

FIGURE 5-8

HOW TO TEACH THE CHILD WITH A
STRONG AUDITORY MODALITY IN THE CLASSROOM

- Talk through large and small muscle motor movements.
- Verbalize the organization of tasks and steps in problem solving.
- Provide a rhythmic structure for motor and reading tasks — work to a beat or a timing pattern.
- Give questions and directions orally and have the child repeat them.
- Let children answer questions orally.
- Have children spell words orally to memorize them or trigger word recognition.
- Teach a phonetic decoding system.
- Playing rhyming and blending word games.
- Have children categorize and sequence words orally with many types of games.
- Read to children to reinforce phonics (Dr. Seuss books), give them information and material about which you can ask comprehension questions.
- Let children read orally often.
- Make frequent use of tape recorders and records of many types.
- Have children write from dictation.

Specific Teaching Suggestions

- Spelling.

  1. Words need to be apart visually and sound units attached to visual units. Example: com   pre   hen   sion.

  2. If child has difficulties with reversals, then a model that he can look at may help his writing.

  3. He may need very definite structure on the page as to where to write his words.

  4. Even though he may hear and analyze a word correctly, difficulties may be present in attaching the sound to the correct visual symbol.Simultaneous looking at, tracing, and saying the sound may help to remediate this problem.

106

- Written language.
  1. May need to give child external structure as to where to put things.
     a. Red lines for margins.
     b. Arrows for indentations.
     c. Colored lines for size and spacing of handwriting.
  2. May have to have punctuation marked, capitalization, etc., explained orally as he/she may not understand or remember on a visual level.
  3. May need to be taught specific ways of checking and monitoring his written work as he probably will not use his visual system to do this.
- Reading.
  1. Use a phonetic or word family approach.
  2. Sight words may be difficult for a child with visual problems, especially visual memory ones. Again a simultaneous auditory, visual, and kinesthetic approach may be useful.
  3. To bridge the gap between letter by letter sounding out and more rapid reading, use a stop watch to time the child's reading. Let him reread for a faster time, thus competing against only himself.
  4. Underlining sound units of a word may help the child learn to look for patterns of letters that make certain sounds.

FIGURE 5-9

HOW TO SPOT THE KINESTHETIC LEARNER IN THE CLASSROOM

- Movers — that is how they learn.
- Want to touch — feel everything.
- Rubs hand along the wall while in lunch line, walking down the hall.
- Puts hand on the door frame. Touches desks as goes down aisles.
- Thumps buddies.
- Often writes everything — over and over.
- Can take gadget apart and put it back together.
- Has many things to play with.
- Enjoys doing things with hands.
- Is not clumsy; good at sports (if visual modality strength is lacking, will be good at those sports where no visual analysis is required).

- Frequently uses fists.
- May be the child who is always making airplanes; fans from paper.

FIGURE 5-10

HOW TO MAKE ADJUSTMENT FOR THE CHILD
WITH KINESTHETIC MODALITY WEAKNESS IN THE CLASSROOM

- Some children with this problem are given medication.

- Make it harder to move than to sit still (place the child's table and chair close to the wall to make him/her aware of movement — he/she may be unaware of his/her own movement. Also, he/she is distracted by movement of others.

- Make certain that these children go to the bathroom, have drinks, etc., before beginning instructional period.

- Don't ask them to sit too long. You will get more out of them in three minutes of concentrated work than in thirty minutes when conditions are not right.

- This child has a need to know when the work/study time will end. A timer or clock is useful.

- Don't place this child too near other children.

- Contingency management system good with this type of child — task-reward.

- Quiet periods interspersed with active periods are best.

- This child needs a quieting-down period after physical activity.

FIGURE 5-11

a small group setting. This can be an extremely valuable in-service experience for many classroom teachers in learning about problem areas in perceptual processing and children's preferred learning styles. It is to be hoped that the classroom teacher and resource teacher, as a team, will be able to observe classroom behaviors and identify the child who is having difficulties with visual processing, auditory processing, and motor processing. Teachers should be able to make regular classroom adjustments to accommodate a child in the area of his/her weakness and also to utilize teaching strategies to reach a child through his/her areas of strength.

HOW TO TEACH THE CHILD WITH STRONG

KINESTHETIC MODALITY IN THE CLASSROOM

- Use movement exploration activities — prepositional concepts as well as addition and subtraction concepts can be taught on the monkey bars.

- Let them clap or tap out numbers, syllables, etc.

- Use number lines on the floor — experience learning — move heavy objects along the number line for more physical feedback.

- Walk patterns of words.

- Use sandpaper letters, felt letters, etc.

- Use Flo pens for more kinesthetic feedback.

- This child may need to talk to self to feel self saying things — gets motor feedback even though he may speak in monotone.

- Do lots of things with eyes shut using 3-D letters (some of these children are taught to read Braille).

- Use all the manipulatives possible.

- Use lots of writing. May need to introduce writing with stencils.

- May need Fernald method teaching words, a visual-auditory, kinesthetic technique.

FIGURE 5-12

WORKING WITH THE CLASSROOM TEACHER

Too often in the past, the resource teacher has become synonymous with the resource room and has primarily operated by withdrawing individual students from regular classrooms for individual or small-group instruction. It is strongly recommended that during the first three years of a child's school career, the resource teachers work with children in the regular classroom rather than withdrawing the child to the resource room.

WORKING IN THE REGULAR CLASSROOM

There are several advantages to this method of operation. First and foremost is that the child is not stigmatized and separated from his/her fellow classmates. The resource teacher and the teacher can work as a team while the resource teacher is in the classroom. They can share information about students more readily and the regular classroom teacher has an opportunity to observe what the resource teacher is doing with students and how she is doing the activities. In addition, many of these activities will be done in a small-group setting. This enables a child with a slight developmental lag in some area to be included in the group with whom the resource teacher is working—a child who would otherwise have no contact with the resource teacher.

Team planning can also include more than the classroom teacher and the resource teacher in this procedure. For example, the music teacher, art teacher, and physical education teacher may all be a part of this team. The program "Integrated Ideas for Language Arts" (see Figure 5-13) is an example of a program to be used in the classroom, as well as the gymnasium.

PRIMARY — KINDERGARTEN

INTEGRATED IDEAS FOR LANGUAGE ARTS

- The Primary child has the following characteristics: He or she is noisy, constantly active, egocentric, imitative, and imaginative. Children of this age need to develop their large muscles, their game skills, and their eye-hand coordination.

- When picking "objectives" for a Physical Education lesson, or for an active learning session in the classroom, these personal qualities should be considered; and whenever possible the needs of the children satisfied.

- Classroom concepts can be reinforced and enriched by activity. Language arts, colors, number concepts, listening skills, concentration, and creativity can all be enhanced by "an active approach to learning."

- The following are sample lesson plans, incorporating color, shapes, beginning action words, knowledge of body parts, and other concepts. These are just sample lessons to build on. Using the "problem solving approach" and following the movement method, introduce moving with changes of speed, levels, and directions. All colors and shapes can be used for "spots." This will reinforce classroom concepts. Language development is very important. All words such as over, under, between, through, in, out, big, small, beside, in front, behind, should be emphasized whenever possible. Constantly challenge the children so they must think before they move.

FIGURE 5-13

Figures 5-14 and 5-15 are suggested first lessons for new Primary-Kindergarten children. This lesson is slightly different in format from other lessons. All lessons must be varied to suit the needs of the individual class. *Teachers must learn to recognize the needs of their own children.*

LESSON PLAN

- Theme   Space (1)
- Grade Level (P)   K-1
- Objectives   To teach person space
                             Teach idea of "spots"
                             Teach color red
                             Beginning of body awareness
- Equipment   A cut-out red circle for every child. These may be placed on the floor for the children.
- Activities   (combined introductory and major activities)

    1. Discuss color and shape of "spot."

    2. Children go and stand beside a red circle that has been well placed by teacher.

    3. Swing arms and then legs to have feeling of own space.

    4. Move around your own "spot" anyway you wish, in as big a circle as you can. (Show children what you mean.)

    5. If all children walk, ask them to see if they can think of another way to move. Then pick up an idea from them, e.g. hop — two feet, one foot. Have all the children do it — ask if they can tell what parts of their body are being used.

    6. Can you think of a way to move around your spot with all your body on the floor? Pick up ideas from the children.

    7. Can you curl up in a small ball on your "spot"?

    8. Can you stretch out flat on your back on your "spot"?

    9. Can you find a way to move yourself around and around while lying on your back?

    10. Crouch beside your "spot." Let's see how much space you have above your "spot." Practice jumping up in the air, landing on toes with bent knees. Stress this immediately.

- Culminating Activity

    Lie on stomach beside "spot." Relax. When touched pick up "spot," tiptoe to door. The word spot has been emphasized throughout lesson.

FIGURE 5-14

LESSON PLAN

- Theme   Space (2)
- Grade Level (P)   K-1
- Objectives   Personal space
                         General space
                         Green Circles
- Equipment   A cut-out green circle for every child.
- Facilities   Gymnasium
- Introductory and Major Activities

  1. Children may try to place their own "green circle spots." Do not start lesson until you have rearranged them as necessary.

  2. Let us see how many ways you can jump <u>over</u> your "spot." Immediately start correcting their landings — on toes, knees bent, land lightly. Concentrate on two-foot take off and landing but be pleased with other variations.

  3. Have children look around gym, taking note of where their spot is placed. "When I say <u>go</u> you are going to move around in all this space — always looking for another empty place. When I say "back to your own spot," go and stand <u>beside</u> your own spot. Do this several times. Then have them walk a few steps — call "STOP." Have them look for an empty space, then say "GO." Do this a number of times.

  4. Can you move around in all this space <u>tall</u>?

  5. Can you move around in all this space <u>small</u>?

  6. This time move any way you wish but when I clap my hands go to your own "spot" and make a big shape over it, etc. Make this seem like a game.

  7. <u>Culminating Activity</u> — Lie down and relax beside own "spot." Have a child be the one to go around and touch them.

FIGURE 5-15

As children get older and progress through the grades, the classroom-based model of service delivery may become much less accepted by the regular classroom teachers. This however, does not change the primary goal of enhancing the child's self-esteem. This must be carefully thought out when the resource teacher is planning a remedial program to be conducted in the resource room, as well as the classroom and home program. It is extremely important that the initial stages of any program contain a great many activities that the child enjoys and can show some measure of success. Later, the more difficult activities for the child can be increased and the enjoyable activities used as a reward for effort.

According to Dr. William Glasser in his discussion of "reality therapy," when children are continuously given tasks at which they do not perceive themselves as succeeding, they consciously "turn off" from attempting those or similar tasks. Therefore, it is extremely important in designing programs for children with learning difficulties that success be planned in the program. This need for success often challenges the creativity and flexibility of the resource teacher's thinking and, at times, may have to be partially found outside the school.

UTILIZING COMMUNITY RESOURCES IN PROGRAMMING

In urban areas, there are many public departments and private organizations that offer specialized programs and give training to their staff members to assist them in dealing with children having "special needs." Among these groups are municipal recreation departments, YMCA's and YWCA's, boy scouts, girl scouts, and many other established youth programs.

In rural areas, this is often not the case. If programs are to be available for children having special needs, they must be either operated by school systems or at least their establishment must be spearheaded by professionals within the school system.

Many excellent programs designed to increase the self-esteem of children and to improve their perceptual functioning have been introduced in recent years. Some have started as local programs and because of their success, have spread not only across local borders, but across national borders. One such excellent program is the Aqua-Percept program, which originated at the community swimming pool in Pointe Claire, Quebec. This program had such outstanding results with children that the Canadian Government, through a variety of grants, funded the dissemination of information about the program. Instructor training courses were offered so that similar programs could be initiated in local communities.

Another such program designed to enhance the self-esteem of young children with learning difficulties is Camp Recskill which has operated in several locations since 1978. This is a summer day camp designed to teach recreational skills to learning disabled children who often have had difficulty finding success in traditional recreation programs, as well as in their school performance.

This camp was designed by one of the authors while a staff member at a mental health center and was a direct extension of personal experience operating a summer program for children with learning difficulties.

While operating the program, the remarkable changes in children's confidence was readily observable. However, the lasting effects of such a program, and whether the children could carry this increased self-esteem back to the classroom, was indeed questionable. In an after-the-fact attempt at evaluating this, permission was granted to review children's grades at the end of the school year prior to attending the summer program, and at the completion of the school year following their participation in the program.

The results were indeed impressive. As a group, the children failed only two subjects while the previous year, they had failed thirty-seven. In addition to this, their grades were raised an average of 19.83 points per student, per subject. The individual results in many cases were even more dramatic. One boy raised his academic average 37 points. Even more impressive however, than the numerical data, was the information supplied by teachers and principals regarding the personality and social development of the children. Most of the children were no longer afraid to attempt new activities and to mix with their peer group.

It is the authors' firm belief that the activities done in the program had little to do with the dramatic improvement in self-esteem. The atmosphere created at the summer program was success oriented and staff were made aware of the fact that effort rather than performance was to be rewarded.

The authors feel that resource teachers must be aware of the availability of such programs in their area and to discuss them with parents as an integral part of the total development of the child. If programs do not exist in your community, special educators can be a catalyst in creating summer camps similar to the one mentioned above.

ROLE OF THE RESOURCE TEACHER WITH OLDER STUDENTS

The role of the resource teacher when assisting students at the upper elementary and secondary school levels must change in emphasis, especially for children who have been on individualized programs with a remedial component for long periods of time. This must be done as the emphasis of curriculum changes from skill acquisition to content.

The resource teacher, in consultation with parents and other school personnel and often with the student involved, must consider a variety of long-term options for each individual student. This planning should entail realistic long-range goal setting as well as the establishment of a variety of short-term goals.

For many students, this may include a variety of programs as alternatives to the traditional academic program. Such long-term goals might include a vocational school program, a cooperative education program, or a work experience program.

For other students having greater academic potential, the resource teacher must assist them in learning ways to compensate for their areas of weaknesses. The resource teacher must also assist secondary school teachers in understanding the specific problems of the student and ways they may accommodate this student in the classroom. Teachers will have to use a variety of methods to assist students in obtaining and retaining information in their subject field as well as the student's ability to process and recall this information for evaluation purposes. Perhaps the greatest use of modern technology in education is in assisting teachers to accommodate students having special needs.

TECHNOLOGY FOR DYSLEXIC AND VISUALLY IMPAIRED STUDENTS

Many volumes have been written regarding the use of microcomputers, both in regular and special education, and certainly these are worthwhile tools for any school system. Because of the capability to use multisensory approaches to learning, computers are particularly useful for learning disabled students having perceptual processing difficulties in one or more areas.

Tape recorders are a valuable tool in assisting the accommodation of students with special needs enabling them to tape their own notes; to tape record assignments and examinations; as well as to receive information by listening to tapes.

Talking books have become very popular during the past few years and have been utilized by dyslexic students as a method to receive information. Students become extremely frustrated at the slow speed of normal tape recordings which have the average speaking speed of approximately 150-175 words per minute. This is only half as fast as the average reading rate of 250-350 words per minute. Much of this frustration can be eliminated by the use of compressed speech. With this technology, tapes can be played at significantly faster speeds than those at which they were recorded and by adjusting the tone, they sound the same as normal speech and not like "Alvin and the Chipmunks." In addition to tapes being played on these variable speed tape recorders, tapes recorded at normal speed can be rerecorded on these recorders and taken home by students to use on their own less expensive machines.

In addition to the variable rate machines, talking encyclopedias will assist students in researching a variety of topics. As a direct result, dyslexic and visually impaired students have been able to remain in straight academic programs and enter universities while still reading at elementary school levels. The use of compressed speech has not only been an advantage for dyslexic students but is also widely used with visually impaired students at both the elementary and secondary levels. One interesting observation is that many students who do not have reading difficulties have been utilizing the machines to assist them with their work because listening is their preferred learning style.

This multifaceted view of the role of the resource teacher is certainly a demanding one, especially in a school system which does not use traditional labels. These various roles of the resource teacher are also a prerequisite if a school system hopes to assist students, previously in full or part-time special classes, to return to the regular classroom and to give them the supports necessary to successfully accomplish this transition. Through assessment, consultation, and direct instruction, resource teachers can be expected to have contact with approximately 15% of the student body. This is certainly an onerous task; however, if the role is remedial instruction, it would be an impossible task.

VOLUNTEER PROGRAMS

One additional facet of the role of the resource teacher is the recruiting, training, and supervision of volunteers utilized for small groups and individual tutoring in the schools.

Volunteers can make significant contributions to individual students, special programs, and school life in general. Volunteers are an excellent way of stretching school resources and assisting the instructional staff in a variety of ways. In addition to this, volunteers are an excellent way of translating the goals and objectives of your programs to the community at large.

Volunteers have been used in many ways within schools (for example: many are used in school libraries, as tutors to individual students, as helpers in classrooms, and in special programs such as swimming programs and class trips). Volunteers may be recruited as individuals or as a group commitment.

One example of the group commitment was observed by the authors many years ago when visiting the Molloy School in Morton Grove, Illinois. The firemen in the City of Morton Grove made a commitment to the school that they would supply one of their members as an assistant to the physical education teacher each day. In Cape Breton County, Nova Scotia, a similar commitment was made by the Royal Canadian Mounted Police, where they supplied two members of their troop each time the highest needs children went swimming.

One great untapped source of volunteers within any school system is students themselves. One of the finest and most comprehensive student volunteer programs is run in the Dade County public schools in Florida. This program is entitled "Turn About ... It's Your Turn to Teach" and is an excellent, comprehensive guide for school systems wishing to start a student volunteer program.

Although there are many advantages in using volunteers, their efforts must be coordinated by the resource teacher. The volunteer is usually unable to do the planning and organization of the program for students and therefore this becomes a major role for the resource teacher. Figure 5-16 is a form that can be utilized by the resource teacher in this organizational process. In addition, this form becomes a permanent record showing what attempts have been utilized to assist students in their areas of need.

The reader can readily see that with the multiplicity of roles played by the effective resource teacher; it takes a very special individual with commitment, skills, creativity, and flexible problem-solving approaches. All school systems have personnel with these characteristics, but for them to be effective and to utilize these abilities, they must feel the support of the board and administration in their efforts. The following short story illustrates this point. (Used with permission of Francis X. MacNeil, Special Education Teacher, Cape Breton District School Board, Sydney, Nova Scotia.)

RESOURCE LESSON PLAN

Student _____   Volunteer and/or _____

School _____   Classroom Teacher _____

Age _____   Resource Teacher _____

Date	Program	Materials	Comments

FIGURE 5-16

DANIEL: AN EDUCATION SUCCESS STORY

The first-time observer would probably find Daniel rather awkward, somewhat uncoordinated, and a slow, labored reader. How, then, could this boy be called an educational success? I believe that success is a relative thing, and as such, it is necessary to look back and see from where the student has come, and what progress he has made. It is only then that we can label Daniel, or anyone else, a success.

After being tested and examined at the Izaak Walton Killam Hospital in Halifax, Daniel was said to be auditorily and visually dyslexic. Translating this into practical terms, it means that he has no strong sensory channel through which he may be able to learn to read. The problems this has caused him are quite obvious, especially when one considers that after spending six years in school, the last of which was in a self-contained special class, he was still a non-reader, with virtually no sight vocabulary.

When these difficulties are considered along with the fact that Daniel's sequential memory and concept of time were vastly underdeveloped, we can come to realize some of his learning difficulties. For example, at 11 years, 5 months of age, he could not read, tell time, did not know the days of the week or the months of the year, and generally had considerable difficulty in most school-related activities. This set of circumstances is even more difficult to understand when one considers that his level of general intelligence (as determined by a standardized individual intelligence test) could be rated as low normal.

Let us now see how Daniel has progressed in order to determine if indeed we can label him a success. At 11 years, 5 months of age, Daniel's sight vocabulary consisted of no more than ten to fifteen words; he could not complete Step 1 of the Dolch list of basic sight words. Now, at the age of 12 years, 0 months, he has worked his way through all eleven steps of the Dolch list, which consists of the 220 most commonly used words. I must clarify the above statement somewhat in order not to give a false impression. Daniel will not immediately recognize all 220 words; however, given an opportunity he can usually now figure out those words that he does not recognize on sight. Also, at times, there is some regression, but generally speaking there has been a steady improvement and I would estimate that he knows, on sight, approximately 75% of the Dolch Basic Word List.

Because of his auditory and visual difficulties in learning words, the approach used to build up his sight vocabulary was the Fernald Technique for learning words, which is a multisensory method of teaching each word to the child. With this, a very basic phonics program was also initiated in order to develop some word attack skills.

When these approaches were combined with additional practice at home, it proved quite successful for Daniel.

Once Daniel had acquired a limited sight vocabulary, a very basic reading program was begun using the words that he had already mastered. The old Ginn Series proved effective in this area until the time was reached when he had gone through the entire list of Dolch words, at which time the Dolch Readers were utilized.

Again, I don't wish to convey a false impression. Daniel is not now a fluent reader and he may never be one, but he can take up a simple text and get through it with a minimum of help, and get some meaning from what he has read. Even at this, there are days when he has great difficulty with words he may have known the previous day; yet he has progressed a long way from not being able to read at all, and from having virtually no sight vocabulary whatsoever.

In the area of his sequential memory, Daniel has progressed quite well. At 12.0 he can now say, in order, the days of the week and the months of the year, as well as being able to single out specific days and months; for example, "What month does the school year begin?" or "What was the day before yesterday?" To these types of questions he responds accurately and with confidence. This success was accomplished through much repetition, and by making him familiar with the use of the calendar.

Daniel can now also tell time with accuracy and again with confidence, although his overall speed at the task could improve. It should be mentioned that he learned this task relatively quickly, which was surprising when one considers that he was reluctant (because of previous failures) even to begin the activity. I must also say that the cooperation at home regarding this particular endeavor, and indeed many others, has been excellent.

This has just been a brief outline of some of the accomplishments of this particular student over the past several months, and in the light of these accomplishments, I feel that he can certainly be called a success.

If this is a success, then I think that it is also important to say why the success happened. In this particular case, the first step was to devise a realistic program for the child which recognized both his capabilities and his limitations. Placement back to the regular classroom was an important part of this first step, and I must state that the cooperation and dedication on the part of the classroom teacher to accommodate this student has been excellent. Daniel does what he is capable of doing with the rest of the Grade 4 class — math, physical education, art, etc., and even participates in a meaningful way in parts of the language arts program such as listening lessons, discussions, etc.

Besides being in the regular classroom for most of the time, Daniel comes out to the resource room four times a week for "his" reading program and extra additional help.

The third part of this success belongs to the parents, who, as mentioned previously, have been most helpful and have always seen that assignments, homework, and other related activities have been carried out.

Without this three-pronged approach to Daniel's problems, I feel that this would not be a success story but only another year of frustration and lack of accomplishment for the student. It is only through this type of cooperation on the part of everyone involved, including Daniel himself, that progress is being made in a realistic way, corresponding to the abilities of the student. Daniel may never appreciate classical literature, yet he will be an adaptive, functional, and productive member of society; and isn't that a success?

CHAPTER 5 REFERENCE MATERIALS

Adams, Norma, "Integrated Ideas for Language Arts," unpublished.

Address: Dartmouth District School Board
               c/o Physical Education Dept.
               95 Victoria Road
               Dartmouth, N.S.
               B3A 1V2

Bluma, Sjetal, *Portage Guide to Early Education*, Portage, Wisconsin, 1976.

Address: Portage Project
               Box 564
               Portage WI 53901

Bush, W. J., and Giles, M. T., *Aids to Psycholinguistic Teaching*, Charles E. Merrill, Co., Columbus, OH, 1969.

Address: Charles E. Merrill Co.
               1300 Alum Creek Drive
               Columbus, OH 43216

Campbell, Wendy, *Aqua Percept*, Pointe-Claire, Quebec, 1976.

Address: Aqua Percept
               Aquatic Department
               98 Douglas Shand Ave.
               Pointe-Claire, Quebec
               H9R 2A8

Address: Continental Press.
               P. O. Box 554
               Elgin, IL 60120

Dade County Public Schools, *Turn About—It's Your Turn to Teach*, Dade County Public Schools, Miami, FL, 1975.

Address: Miami-Dade Community College, North Campus
               11380 N.W. 27th Ave.
               Miami, FL 33167

Developmental Learning Materials.

Address: 7440 Natchez Avenue
               Niles, IL 60648

Dubnoff, Belle; Chambers, Irene; and Schaefer, John; *Dubnoff School Program Series*, Teaching Systems and Resources Inc., Hingham, MA, 1968.

Address: 50 Pond Park Rd.
               Hingham, MA 02043

Educational Insights, *Unique Math Games: 150 Exciting Math Games*, Educational Insights, Inc., Inglewood, CA, 1971.

Educational Insights, *The Reading Box: 150 Reading Games and Activities*, Educational Insights, Inc., Inglewood, CA, 1971.

Address: Educational Insights, Inc.
                423 South Hindry Ave.
                Inglewood, CA 90301

Frostig, Marianne, *Frostig Visual Perception Program*, Follett Publishing Co., Chicago,
    1973.
Address: Follett Publishing Co.
                1010 W. Washington Blvd.
                Chicago, IL 60607

Glasser, William, *Schools Without Failure*, Harper & Row, New York, 1975.
Address: Harper & Row, Publishers
                10 E. 53rd St.
                New York, NY 10022

MacNeil, Francis X., "Daniel: An Education Success Story," *Journal of Education*,
    Nova Scotia Department of Education, Halifax, Nova Scotia, 1981.
Address: Nova Scotia Department of Education
                P. O. Box 578
                Halifax, N.S.
                B3J 2S9

Manolson, Ayala, *It Takes Two to Talk: A Hanen Early Language Parent Guide Book*,
    Hanen Early Language Resource Centre, Toronto, 1983.
Address: Hanen Early Language Resource Centre
                48 Roxborough St., West
                Toronto, Ontario
                M5R 1T8

Novakovich, H., Smith, J., and Tecgardey C., *Target on Language*, Christ Church
    Child Center, Bethesda, MD, 1973.
Address: 8011 Old Georgetown Rd.
                Bethesda, MD 20014

O'Brien, Mary Consilia, Sr., *The Non-Coping Child*, Academic Therapy Publications,
    Novato, CA, 1978.
Address: Academic Therapy Publications
                20 Commercial Boulevard
                Novato, CA 94947

Pipers Program.
Address: Readers Digest Association Inc.
                Customer Service
                Pleasantville, NY 10570

Rutledge, Earl, "Application of Audiotutorial Teaching Utilizing Rate Controlled
    Speech Technologies," unpublished, 1983.
Address: Mr. Earl Rutledge, Teachers' Centre, L.C.D.S.B.
                P. O. Box 380
                Bridgewater, N.S.
                B4V 2W9

Schirmer, Gene, *Performance Objectives for Preschool Children*, Delta Schoolcraft Intermediate School District, Gladstone, MI, 1974.

Address: Delta-Schoolcraft Intermediate School District
                Gladstone, MI 49837

Valett, Robert E., *The Remediation of Learning Disabilities: A Handbook of Psychoeducational Resource Programs*, Fearon, Belmont, CA, 1967.

Address: Fearon Publishing Co.
                P. O. Box 741
                Belmont, CA 94002

CHAPTER 6

Building Special Class Curriculum Based on Goals and Objectives

In nothing do men more nearly approach the Gods
than in doing good for their fellowmen.

Cicero

Historically, special classes in school systems were placed in basements, had poorly trained teachers, and had little or no interaction with other students in the school. Thankfully, all of these things have changed.

During the past decade, the authors have been employed in school districts having an excess of 8,500 students. During this time period, no student was excluded from a school program regardless of functional level. This included students living in institutions because they were unable to be maintained at home. The vast majority of students with special needs can receive a quality educational program within the regular classroom. In order to accomplish this the classroom teacher needs support with the following:

- assessment of learning strengths and needs;
- individualized program design;
- specialized equipment;

- appropriate materials;

- tutoring assistance (e.g. volunteers, tutors, or resource teacher);

- teacher aide, if required (e.g. toileting, feeding, etc.);

- support from administration and specialists;

- assistance in evaluation.

Some students will need a more restrictive placement in order to receive a quality program. Refer to the Cascade Model in Chapter 1. The danger is placing a student in an environment that is more restrictive than necessary. Most students requiring special academic programs can cope in regular homerooms and can benefit socially from placement in regular physical education, art, and music classes. Many of these students can take some academic courses in regular classrooms with only minor modifications.

High needs classes are part-time special classes and the role of the special class teacher is to organize the educational programs of those students who have been assigned to her or his class. Students are mainstreamed into regular classes where possible. All students are placed in regular homerooms and spend only 25 percent to 75 percent of their school day with the special class teacher.

For the understanding of the reader, some examples of students referred to as high needs are those who are traditionally labeled:

- Educable Mentally Handicapped

- Severely Learning Disabled

- Emotionally Handicapped

- Culturally Deprived

A small number of students require an even more restrictive placement. These students are the ones we refer to as highest needs students. Some traditional labels for these students are:

- Trainable Mentally Handicapped

- Autistic

- Multiply Handicapped

- Severely Emotionally Disturbed

Highest needs students spend the vast majority of their time in a special class with their teacher and teacher aides. These students are integrated with regular classes for as many school activities as possible. Volunteers are extremely valuable for integrating these students into community activities.

These classifications or placements are based on student need and level of independent functioning at a given time. Ongoing review and evaluation is important to enable the students to move toward a less restrictive environment. This move should be based on the acquisition of skills and behavior needed to be successful in a less restrictive placement.

Altering student placement can be done at any time during the school year to ensure that each student is in the most productive environment as possible.

SPECIAL CLASS CURRICULUM

Curriculum designed for the special needs of these students has also changed; however, it is still basically a curriculum designed by professionals with little recognition of long-term goals and objectives. Certainly, if mainstreaming, based on the "least restrictive environment," is the model for the service delivery, then the major goal and objective is to continually move children toward the most normal setting. There will, however, always be children who will need special classes during the entire course of their school career.

Too often these children continue in an academically oriented program for too long a period of time, leaving much too short a period of time to work on life skills necessary to function as an adult in the community. Honest and frequent communication is needed between school and parents in order to make the best possible decisions about placement and program for students in special classes. This of course is true about all students, but has more significance in the case of students in either full- or part-time special classes.

UTILIZING PARENTS IN CURRICULUM PLANNING

In order for the student to receive maximum benefit from the program during school years, home and school must agree on the objectives and goals of this program. It is certainly not unusual to have parents of individual students meeting with school personnel and in some places it is required by law. In addition to this however, there are many advantages of having meetings involving groups of parents to discuss more universal issues. Often in urban areas, this is done through associations. Unfortunately, in many rural areas of North America, these associations are not active and if such meetings are to take place, they usually must be initiated by the school system.

There are also many advantages of having group parent meetings. First of all, other parents can be a great source of strength and information to parents going through a particularly troublesome time with their "special needs" child. Parents can often become valuable volunteers within the system and can be of great assistance in establishing new and needed programs. When planning curriculum however, parents are too often ignored in the process of establishing what the goals and objectives of their children's programs should be.

The authors have recently gone through a very interesting process with groups of parents and teachers working together to achieve consensus on goals and objectives for both high needs students and highest needs students. It must be emphasized that the *process is the important aspect.* A complete understanding of the process, goals, and objectives, as well as the curriculum guides that evolved, will be explained later in this chapter.

The process started by having meetings of all the high needs teachers and companion meetings of all of the highest needs teachers along with central office staff. The teachers represented all of the age levels within the system, which added to program continuity, from ages five to twenty-one. The meetings continued until consensus was reached among the teachers on the goals and objectives for each age group of students. The goals and objectives were established in five areas:

- academic goals and objectives;
- recreational goals and objectives;
- prevocational and vocational goals and objectives;
- social and emotional goals and objectives;
- life skills goals and objectives.

Following these meetings, the goals and objectives outlined by the teachers were sent home to parents well in advance of meetings which were held in each locale involving parents, teachers, principals, and central office staff and school board members. At the meetings, parents were encouraged to comment on the goals and objectives and to make suggestions for additions or deletions. The meetings also gave parents an opportunity to seek clarification and to allow staff to relate specific activities in their program as it related to the goals and objectives for students.

Following the parent meetings, the teachers again met and developed curriculum guides to meet these goals and objectives. The guides discussed strategies, methodology, and specific materials that they had found helpful when meeting similar goals and objectives in their program. Teachers found this especially helpful in a rural area with great distances between schools. Teachers have also found that there was not a great deal of opportunity for interaction among teachers having students with similar needs at similar age levels. The teachers learned a great deal from each other, especially regarding strategies and materials that they used in their own schools. The reader must again be cautioned that the process was the important learning experience for the teachers involved.

Following are the curriculum guides incorporating the goals and objectives for both highest and high needs students developed through this process. Although these guides are general, they enable the teacher to have a basic framework within which to develop individual programs for each child. The teacher's knowledge of the individual child and his/her learning style will enable the teacher to select the most appropriate materials for assisting the child to reach the stated goals and objectives. There should also be some leeway when moving a child from one age-level class to another. This determination will be made through consultation with teachers and parents. (For the reader's convenience, suppliers of materials are listed in the reference section at the end of this chapter.)

CURRICULUM GUIDE FOR HIGHEST NEEDS STUDENTS

I. Five- to Eleven-Year-Olds

- *Academic Goals*

    1. Develop basic perceptual skills for academic readiness

        (a) perceptual motor skills

        (b) auditory perception skills

        (c) language skills (expressive and receptive)

        (d) visual discrimination skills

        (e) memory skills (auditory, visual, and motor)

    2. Develop basic academic skills (for those who have achieved readiness)

This is a developmental period of time when teachers will continually assess students and attempt to understand their learning style so that each child will be able to be taught most effectively through his strengths, while at the same time attempting to build up his particular areas of weakness in order to assist him in progressing as rapidly as possible.

The programs and activities utilized to accomplish these goals are listed below:

Distar Reading;
Sullivan Reading;
Distar Math;
Radea;
Russell Sorting;
DLM Auditory Program;
Dubenoff Program;
DLM Pegs;
Individual Journals and Free Time Reading;
Reading Toy Box;
Foundations for Mathematics;
Frostig Program;
The New Exploring Science Yellow Book;
Pittman Learning Program;
Chime-In;
Peabody Preschool and Primary Language Program.

In addition to this, a variety of movement programs are used in conjunction with the physical education staff and volunteers.

● *Recreational Goals and Objectives*

1. To improve movement skills

2. To improve spatial awareness

3. To improve general physical fitness

4. To learn cooperative play skills

5. To achieve readiness for group, athletic, and recreational activities

The majority of these young students are behind, academically and in all areas of development. Therefore, it is important to improve movement skills, awareness of themselves, and their position in space. They must learn sharing, taking turns, and staying with an activity so that they may learn these skills in order to be integrated into a variety of activities with their peer group in regular classes.

In order to accomplish this, the following programs and activities are utilized:

The Radea Program;

The Willows Program from Piper;

Specific developmental movement activities carried out every day both in the classroom and in the gymnasium, as well as combined gym activities for many of the students with regular class students;

Special times set aside for skating, bowling and practice for Special Olympics;

All highest needs students have an organized swimming and aquatics program to assist them in their movement skills and general physical fitness;

A variety of organized games are played within the classroom to achieve cooperative play skills in a controlled environment;

Parents are encouraged to enroll their children in nonschool recreational activities that have adult leadership.

● *Vocational and Prevocational Goals*

1. Awareness of the world of work (career infusion)

2. Developing good work habits

Vocational and prevocational work is a minimal and incidental part of their program: however, there are many discussions of roles and occupations that occur in stories, field trips to a variety of community resources, and some films and tapes that discuss jobs as part of the overall story.

An emphasis is made to develop good work habits during this important developmental phase for our highest needs children, as these habits will assist them not only throughout their academic career, but later in life in their vocational career.

- *Social and Emotional Goals*
    1. To develop self-awareness and self-confidence
    2. Develop trust of the adults in their environment
    3. To develop socially acceptable behaviors
    4. Develop awareness and appropriate methods of expressing emotions

This area is perhaps the most important developmental area for all students. There are many individuals in the world who are not academically skilled but all must have social and emotional awareness in order to be accepted by other individuals in their life. In order to accomplish these goals, special emphasis is placed on communication skills, sharing work together, respecting adults and peers, delivering messages, proper answering of the telephone, learning to get around the school, and going to and from the bus with less and less supervision. A special effort is made on developing proper eating habits, passing food carefully and a variety of self-help skills. Age-appropriate self-control of emotions without a denial of this emotion is important. Emphasis is placed on following through on tasks, whether they be assigned or of choice.

Specific programs that are utilized to meet these objectives are the Radea Program, the Peabody Language Program, and sharing of games within the classroom.

Having a variety of parties, sharing treats, and special playtimes in the classroom are important. A special effort has also been made to take one or two children to a variety of community activities and to encourage parents and volunteers to do the same, so that assessment, monitoring, and carry-over of learned social skills can be achieved.

- *Life Skills Goals and Objectives*
    1. To develop good personal hygiene habits
    2. To develop age-appropriate communication skills
    3. To develop problem solving techniques
    4. To learn to share in responsibility for maintenance of classroom
    5. To develop acceptable eating habits
    6. To develop skills to be integrated with regular classes for activities where possible

Special emphasis is placed on life skills, because many of these self-help skills are needed to accomplish the goal of integrating these students as much as possible with their age mates throughout the school. Self-help skills and practice include complete care of their outer clothing (including boots), dressing and undressing, getting ready for bed alone at home and dressing for school with as little help as possible. An attempt is made to instill the idea of time, to follow through on tasks of their own choice, and to accept a change of routine with some warning.

It is extremely important to develop good communication between home and school so that many of the life skills that are worked on in school can be reinforced at home. Some skills are necessary also for smooth operation of the school program of the students. For example, many of our activities include getting ready for gym, swimming, bowling, and skating. Some activities in the life skills area of the Radea Kit also give many ideas for assisting children with general life skills.

II. Twelve- to Seventeen-Year-Olds (Highest Needs Students)

● *Academic Goals and Objectives*

1. To develop basic reading, writing, and math skills to functional level

2. To develop study and learning skills

3. To develop work habits

4. To enjoy and appreciate learning

At this age level, students must begin to think and act appropriately for themselves in an academic setting, to make more of their own decisions, to analyze their own problem solving, and to be instructed in other methods of problem solving. Every attempt will be made to improve students' academic skills in the areas of reading, comprehension, and mathematics in order to assist them to function independently in society.

Programs and materials utilized to assist students at this level include in the Reading and Language Arts area:

The Job Ahead;
Multiple Skills Series;
Using the Context;
Working with Sounds;
Focus on Phonics;
Great Short Stories;
Word Puzzles;
Hayes Language Skills;
My First Stories;
Handmade worksheets.

In the area of mathematics, materials used are Mafex Addition, Multiplication, and Division; handmade worksheets; the calculator; math word problems; Basic Counting.

More specifically in the area of math, time will be an important factor for functional living. Materials used in developing concepts of time are:

What Time Is It?

Bingo;

Handmade time worksheets;

A manipulative clock.

For students not yet understanding the time concepts of months, days, and the use of the calendar, this will continue to be a priority. Also in the area of mathematics, a great deal will be done with the use of money utilizing handmade worksheets, play money, making change, and buying items in practice and real-life situations.

- *Recreational Goals and Objectives*

  1. To improve muscle tone, coordination, stability, and flexibility, for those students who require this basic physical development

  2. To increase the level of physical fitness of students

  3. To participate in organized activities both as individuals and as part of a team

  4. To expose students to a variety of recreational activities and to learn how to utilize these activities within their community

  5. To participate in special olympics activities to enable them to become part of a team and share in team responsibilities such as giving their best in participation, and proper behavior and responsibility when traveling

Various activities and programs are utilized to accomplish the above goals with this age group. These students participate in bowling, swimming, and skating, which also assists them in a great many self-help skills and life skills. This exposes them to a variety of activities in the community, and how to access facilities. Each student has three weekly periods of physical education, where they participate in both individual and group sports and are able to practice specific sports skills for participation in Special Olympics programs. Many other recreational interests are pursued through the school program, such as art, music, crafts, and collecting. Camping is an important part of the program where children again must combine many skills that they learn during their time in class to effectively look after their own self-help needs.

- *Vocational and Prevocational Goals and Objectives*

  1. To understand the importance of work in establishing adult independence

  2. To learn a variety of careers through curricular activities

  3. To develop an appreciation for the dignity of work

  4. To experience a variety of possible employment situations and exposure to skills needed to secure and maintain a position in the work force

This is an important area for the oldest students in this age group. Although it is still basically prevocational, it is important for them to be aware of the world of work since many of their age peers are being prepared to enter the work force. The programs and activities utilized to meet these goals and objectives are:

1. a variety of workbooks dealing with jobs, job interviews, and job applications;

2. dealing with a variety of words on job applications and learning how to properly print a variety of appropriate responses.

In addition to this, there are visits to a variety of community resources such as open and sheltered employment centers, and government employment agencies. Students have an opportunity to proceed with mock interviews, discussing proper dress and appropriate responses to questions during interviews. They discuss paychecks and deductions and the necessity for these deductions in our society. A variety of discussions take place, both planned and spontaneous, concerning the value of work and its importance in life.

- *Social and Emotional Goals and Objectives*
    1. To develop self-understanding and acceptance
    2. To recognize that all individuals have strengths and weaknesses
    3. To improve their own self concept
    4. To develop socially acceptable behaviors
    5. To develop healthy attitudes about human sexuality and understand the difference between appropriate private and public behaviors

The social and emotional goals and objectives basically permeate all parts of the curriculum. Many of our students have a poor self-image and self-concept because of their interactions with other people in the past. Therefore we do many things to help improve their own self-image. In addition to this, a great deal of positive reinforcement is given to acceptable behaviors and discussions about unacceptable behaviors that the students exhibit in order to better assist them to the social milieu of the school and the community. We specifically attempt to give students proper information about human sexuality and to discuss with them appropriate private and public behaviors. Some of the specific programs and activities utilized to meet these objectives are planned discussions, student involvement in groups with specific assignments within the school setting, health and sex education programs, spontaneous discussions following classroom or school incidents, and utilization of materials such as the Feeling Good Cards.

- *Life Skills Goals and Objectives*
    1. To develop self-sufficient personal hygiene habits
    2. To develop problem communication skills

3. To develop problem solving techniques

4. To develop good health, safety, and first aid skills

5. To develop a good sense of values

6. To learn about and utilize community resources

It is important for the students to develop independence appropriate to their individual developmental age; for example, activities are done to emphasize cleanliness of self and clothing, as well as the skills necessary to maintain these at a high level. Teachers in school assist the boys with industrial arts projects and the girls with home economics where they learn a variety of skills that will help them in independent living. Many of the recreational activities involve a great deal of life skills practice as do some of the specific curricular materials involved in the academic programs. All students do a great many errands and use facilities both within and outside the school such as trips to the office, the elementary school, the post office, the police station, the bank, the store, the mall, the women's center, the laundromat, the arena, the bowling alley, the bus station, the sheltered workshop, the park and museum, and other community facilities.

III. Eighteen- to Twenty-One-Year-Olds (Highest Needs Students)

A program based on goals and objectives for 18- to 21-year-old highest needs students is the "Verge House Program." This program is a complete life skills program and is conducted in a beautiful old home adjacent to the elementary school and the junior-senior high school in town.

Initially, the reader may feel that this is contrary to the philosophy of mainstreaming. In discussions with professionals and parents, it was felt that 18- to 21-year-old highest needs students must be integrated into community life and not into the student life of the junior-senior high school. The staff has found this program to be extremely rewarding. Many adults in the community, on a voluntary basis, help students develop their interests in art, music, crafts, sewing, and home living skills.

The students are completely responsible for the upkeep of the house and receive no janitorial services. This includes shoveling snow, cutting grass, cleaning, washing, painting and wallpapering. Each week, the students do comparative pricing, do their grocery shopping, and prepare a cooked noon meal. Also on Fridays, a formal dinner is prepared and guests are invited to the home to be served a meal. There are only six guests invited each Friday, usually a parent, a volunteer, a school board or central office staff member, and a variety of citizens from businesses throughout the district. This has proven to be beneficial for the development of restaurant training skills and appropriate social behaviors.

Although this is a school program, occasionally, students do stay overnight with staff members at the home to learn specific skills. The location of the Verge House is within easy access to major recreational facilities in the town, such as ice skating, curling, and swimming. It is also close to a variety of work experience placements, both competitive and sheltered, and within easy access to the major shopping area. With this close proximity to the elementary school, those students capable of working as teacher assistants in the elementary school are placed there for periods of time. These placements have been valuable in increasing the self-esteem of students by placing them in the "helper" role rather than the role of always being helped.

The major goals of this program are:

- *Academic Goals and Objectives*

     1. To do activities to reinforce present academic skills

     2. To relate academic skills to general life skills and occupational skills

Because students are moving into their last level of public school education, the emphasis on pure academics is minimized and the application of present academic skills to functional living and employment is stressed.

- *Recreational Goals and Objectives*

     1. Choosing their own leisure time activities

     2. Exposing a variety of leisure time activities (with an emphasis on life long activities)

     3. Stressing the value of physical fitness

     4. Learning about the recreational and leisure time facilities in their own community and how to access them

It is extremely important for students at this age to begin to make their own decisions and their leisure time activities. In the future they will have a great deal of leisure time which should bring them joy, and help assist them into community life. In order to accomplish this, a variety of individuals from the community contribute to the program by teaching leisure time skills. Also, numerous outside school events are planned to enable them to become familiar with activities in their community. Some of the activities utilized are ice skating, roller skating, outdoor ice skating, bowling, curling, movies, card games, arts and crafts, and making Christmas and birthday presents for family and friends. In addition to this, a great many of the students enjoy being involved in more active Special Olympics activities and a variety of exercise programs such as swimming, yoga, and relaxation exercises. Many hobbies are initiated and encouraged during this time of the student's life such as growing plants, painting, reading, cooking, music, board games, and listening to taped stories.

Students are given the opportunity to organize a variety of activities such as birthday parties, Halloween parties, Christmas parties, and tea and craft sales. Students are encouraged to become involved in community groups with which they share a common interest, such as art, karate, hiking, etc. It is hoped that through exposure and participation in a variety of activities, students will learn some of the skills necessary to maintain these leisure time interests following their school career and throughout their life.

- *Vocational and Prevocational Goals and Objectives*

    1. To obtain full-time employment either competitive or sheltered (at the end of their program)
    2. To master the steps necessary to apply for and retain a job
    3. To understand and appreciate the value and dignity of work
    4. To develop an understanding of how the employment system operates
    5. To understand their own employment strengths and weaknesses
    6. To demonstrate all of the above through successful work experience

It is hoped that at the end of their program, all of our students will be assisted into a job placement within the community or in a sheltered workshop setting. During their program, all students will have a variety of work experience placements geared to their own readiness level. Out-of-school resources utilized are training centers, sheltered workshops, as well as a variety of community work experience placements such as hospitals, motels, florist shops, laundromats, veterinarians' offices, hardware stores, nursing homes, restaurants, and positions with private businesses in the agricultural, forestry, and fishing industries.

The in-school program designed to assist and precede the work experience contains the following elements: money management and banking; communication skills; use of the telephone; kitchen management; time management; following established work routines; filling out applications; proper dress and behavior during interviews; utilizing transportation systems; and doing laundry, housecleaning, house maintenance, outdoor yard work, etc.

Meaningful reading vocabulary and general social skills are stressed. Total maintenance of the Verge House and its grounds are their responsibility as well as planning and organizing the daily routine of the house and special events that take place there. When students are ready for work experience, they must go through all the procedures of getting a regular job such as filling out applications and having job interviews.

- *Social and Emotional Goals and Objectives*

    1. To develop socially acceptable adult behavior
    2. To understand and successfully deal with their own emotions
    3. To understand and assert their own individual rights
    4. To understand and appropriately deal with their own sexuality
    5. To understand, accept, and like themselves and others

This primary goal of teaching socially acceptable behavior is done by utilizing information gained from adaptive behavior scales and program activities based on adaptive and maladaptive behaviors. Part of the difficulty is lack of confidence and experience in social situations. Some of this is improved by activities such as dealing with others in the kitchen and in doing jobs around the house. In addition to this, special guest luncheons give students an opportunity to introduce themselves and their skills to the community and receive positive reinforcement for their efforts.

- *Social and Emotional Goals and Objectives*

A variety of self-concept materials are used in the program. The use of videotaping to show students maladapted behaviors is utilized as well as task analysis with information from the SAIL and SCIL programs. Students are exposed to relaxation techniques and appropriate emotional outlets such as art, music, and sports. A variety of materials and methods used to assist students in achieving these goals are in the area of community studies, sex education, what I do best, the Feeling Good cards, and competency based strengths assessments. Of course, much of the milieu of the house allows for interaction and evaluation of social/emotional adjustment and maladjustment.

- *Life Skills Goals and Objectives*

  1. To learn to live as independently as possible (i.e. group home or supervised apartment)
  2. To develop self-sufficient personal hygiene
  3. To understand good nutrition principles
  4. To develop proper communication skills
  5. To develop problem solving techniques
  6. To develop good health, safety, and first aid skills
  7. To develop a good sense of values
  8. To learn about and utilize community resources
  9. To understand personal learning strengths and weaknesses

One of the primary reasons for the existence of the Verge House is to be able to teach group home living skills so that students, upon completion of the program, can be integrated into group homes and/or supervised apartments. Another primary objective is to enable students to be integrated, as much as possible, with adults in the community. Part of the integration is done by bringing adults into the home for specific purposes. Some of the programs and materials utilized for achieving basic goals are SAIL and SCIL programs, including self-help skills, toilet use, eating manners, cleanliness, care of personal property, eliminating unacceptable vocal and facial mannerisms, etc. Where possible, the students use activities for the development of self-direction, independence, specific vocational training, and accepting responsibility in the leadership of group activities. Much use is made of the adaptive behavior scale and this can be easily transferred into individualized programs for each student, with periodic evaluations to measure progress and current program needs. It is in the life skills area that many volunteers from the community are essential in helping the teaching staff with individualized instruction. Responsibility for home maintenance is important in building self-esteem as well as in teaching the skills required. Students are also required to plan and prepare nutritious meals. They do comparative shopping, preparing, serving, and clean-up for these meals. Many of the students take the responsibility for organizing and coordinating group activities both within the house and in the community. A great emphasis is placed on reasoning skills and making independent decisions.

Programs and materials utilized to assist students at this level include:

SAIL — Skills to Achieve Independent Living

SCIL — Systematic Curriculum for Independent Living

Reading Labels and Signs

Lauback Way to Reading

My Book of Workers

Mafex Math Survival Series

Radea — Testing and Remediation

Feeling Good About Yourself — A Guide for Working with People Who Have Disabilities

Feeling Good Cards

The Teenage Survival Book

Sound Filmstrip, *I Can Say No*

Prevocational Tool Assembly Kit

CURRICULUM GUIDE FOR HIGH NEEDS STUDENTS

Five-to Eight-Year-Olds

● *Academic Goals and Objectives*

1. Reentry to full-time regular class as rapidly as possible.
2. Building up academic skills to maximize potential in the following areas:
   a. perceptual efficiency
   b. communication skills (reading, writing, speaking, and listening)
   c. mathematics skills

This academic program designed for each child must be based on the student's rate and style of learning and at the same time, integrate him/her as much as possible into the regular classroom setting. It is important that continuous evaluation be a part of each program so that as soon as a child is ready to cope in regular classes, he/she is moved in as rapidly as possible. Because of the amount of time that the students spend in regular classrooms, it is important to have frequent meetings between the Special Education teacher and the regular classroom teacher.

Listed below are a variety of programs and activities that are utilized to meet these goals and objectives:

1. *Language*

    Whole Language, Big Books and Language Experience

    Methuen Readers

    Low Vocabulary — High interest books such as *Thunder the Dinosaur*

    Books and Monster Books

    Dolch Sight Word List

    Library Materials

    Fernald Program

    Partner Reading through the Regular Class programs

    Piper Program

    Peabody Language Development Kits — Levels P and 1

    Various workbooks and teacher made activities to develop skills

    Instant Language Builders

    Resource Book for the Special Education Teacher

    Multiple Skills Series (Reading Kit)

Other school staff who participate in language programs are the regular classroom teachers, special education aide, speech therapist, and librarian.

2. *Mathematics*

    Manipulative materials

    D.L.M. materials

    Teaching Math to the Learning Disabled

    Computerized math programs

3. *Visual*

    Piper Program

    D.L.M. materials and other assorted programs and activities used to develop skills such as visual motor, figure-ground, spatial relations;

position in space and visual memory.

Regular classroom teachers, parents, the art teacher, Special Education aide, and volunteers help in these activities.

4. *Auditory*

Piper Program

Perceive and Respond, A Variety of Auditory Programs

Assorted materials and programs

Auditory activities are utilized in the Special Education and regular classroom, at home, and by volunteers.

5. *Gross Motor and Body Movement and Awareness*

Piper Program

Aqua Percept

Physical education classes

Other assorted activities

Gross motor programming includes help from volunteers, Special Education aide, and physical education teachers.

6. *Social/Emotional*

Social Learning Curriculum

● *Recreational Goals and Objectives*

This program enables the child to participate fully in peer-oriented activities and to make productive use of leisure time.

1. Recreational skill development

2. Develop leisure time pursuits that are age appropriate

3. Develop physical fitness and movement skills

This area of a child's development is extremely important and must be done in consultation with parents since many of the activities could be misunderstood by parents as not being academic in nature. Also, it is important to stress activities to benefit the child that will be done outside of school hours requiring parental permission and involvement. Many of these activities are important to instill feelings of self-confidence, enjoyment, and a feeling of belonging in students who, because of academic and developmental weaknesses, must be singled out in a school setting for specialized help.

The programs and activities that are utilized to meet these recreational goals and objectives are as follows:

1. Aqua Percept Program — becoming confident in using the community

pool and developing various skills necessary to meet the goals listed above (this is a weekly program).

2. Bowling, ice skating, roller skating, organizing Christmas dinner and parties, annual class trip.

3. Extracurricular activities are available to all students. Many take place at noontime and are available to Special Education students; i.e., dance class, floor hockey, art club, music, and intramurals.

4. Specialist subjects such as physical education, music, art, and library, also encourage leisure time activities and help develop many other skills.

5. Community activities such as Girl Scouts, Beavers, Gymnastics, etc., are encouraged especially for children who may be having difficulties meeting and interacting with others.

6. Camp Recskill — A specialized summer day camp for 6- to 10-year olds.

- *Prevocational Skills*

  - To develop a sense of the value and dignity of work.

    a. to foster good work habits

    b. career infusion through regular curriculum materials

With this age group of children, many activities that happen within the regular classroom make them aware of the variety of occupations available within the community through curricular stories and materials as well as visitors to the classroom and field trips throughout the years. It is important for the teacher, parents, and other adults dealing with the children to keep a positive approach regarding the dignity of work in all jobs and occupations. It is also important to assist students in developing skills necessary for success in future occupations and occupational training programs by stressing the following factors: following directions; completing assigned tasks; following established routines; developing a sense of responsibility; developing good communications skills; developing the ability to work both independently and with others; and developing academic skills necessary for placement into a vocational program.

- *Social and Emotional Goals and Objectives*

  - To enhance self-concept and self-esteem.

    a. assisting children in learning how to interpret social cues and develop appropriate responding behaviors

    b. providing socializing opportunities

    c. educating significant others

    d. providing direct instruction in these areas

This area is extremely important with children to begin to help them understand, identify, and to deal in a socially acceptable way with various emotions through a variety of planned experiences. School boards that have adopted the model of mainstreaming by placing children in the least restrictive environment, have made the most significant decision for the positive social and emotional growth for children requiring Special Education services.

Mainstreaming encourages strengthening of self concept; access to valued peer models; more learning and socializing opportunities; greater likelihood of normal and higher expectations; more changes for autonomy and independence; and, most important, it helps children in the regular stream understand and accept Special Education students by their realization that they are more similar to themselves than they are different.

Parents are included to a great extent in programming for their children's social and emotional needs. They are encouraged to help their child deal positively with his or her limitations and with the development of their strengths.

Agencies such as Family and Childrens' Services, Mental Health, Big Brother, etc., are utilized as support systems for families who are experiencing difficulties at home which may be affecting a child's growth.

- *Life Skills Goals and Objectives*
    - To achieve age-appropriate self-help skills
        a. personal hygiene and grooming
        b. health and nutrition habits
        c. safety and survival skills
        d. domestic skills

This guideline has previously mentioned that many of these students are behind, not only in academic skills, but in a variety of developmental areas. It is imperative to assist them with general life skills, as this will enable them to fit into regular classes, recreation, and social programs with students not having academic and other difficulties. The acquisition of age-appropriate life skills makes integration into the mainstream of school and community life a simpler process. It is important for students in Special Education to have the opportunity for direct teaching and practice of these skills.

Activities to Be Practiced to Reach These Goals and Objectives

Dressing and undressing

Personal hygiene skills

Cooking and using proper eating habits; Using the telephone; and, Getting around the community.

Health and Nutrition Units of Study

Safety and Survival Curriculum Guides

Nine- to Thirteen-Year-Olds (High Needs Students)

- *Academic Goals and Objectives*

  1. to improve mathematics skills

  2. to improve communication skills

  3. to improve perceptual efficiency

  4. to work on general information acquisition in such areas as science and social studies

  5. to develop functional academics: the everyday application of academic knowledge and skills

This age seems to be a critical point in which parents and students must make decisions regarding future choices in education. For many students who are able to fit into the regular classroom in academic areas, this should be their last opportunity to really push for skill improvement. For those students who seem to be falling further behind, regardless of the amount of time spent, this can be a time in which academics be deemphasized. These students and their parents need to be aware of the variety of programs available at the secondary level.

Programs and Activities Utilized to Meet These Objectives

1. Language Arts Skills — reading groups plus novel study, spelling groups, functional spelling.

   - Reading: basal readers, individual word lists, Dolch word lists, novel studies for older children, real stories, Cracking the Code, other linguistic readers, Sullivan Program Reading, whole language approaches, target words for functional reading towards development of employable skills, Specific Skills Series, questions, main ideas, dictionary skills, etc.

   - Written Expression and Writing Skills: journals, writing personal information, calendar, cursive writing program (blackboard to pen-paper at desk), learning to copy from blackboard, Vanguard, Dubnoff.

   - Spelling: Ves Thomas, I Can Spell, Fernald approach, blackboard activities.

   - Communcation and Language Skills: Distar Language (group approach), verb usage expansion and elaboration method, conversation time, speech therapy services.

2. Mathematical Skills — individualized (levels range from Grade 1 to Grade 5).

   - Concept development: counters, aids, Mathematics Their Way, Work Jobs, Key Math cubes.

- Computation: Health program, Spectrum, Project Math, Enright Diagnostic Test — error analysis used to develop programs, Sullivan Program Math.

- Application: time telling, money, card games, board games, Mott's Life Skills Application, grocery lists, story problems, adaptations, calculators, Chisanbop, math charts, pegboard designs, group math games, Precision Math.

3. General Information — Science — scientific method, social and community studies, local history projects, community work projects, community service projects.

4. Functional Academics — Time, money handling skills, story problems, reading schedules, purchasing ability, danger words, transportation signs, grocery word lists, community signs, telephone directory skills, personal information reporting, newspaper skills, calendar, basic geography skills, and measurement.

5. Adaptions to programs — use of tape recorder, language master, computer, calculator reading, math skills and concepts in relation to:

   concrete experiences, behavioral management techniques;

   games, circle meetings;

   peer tutoring, hearing impaired tutor;

   perceptual motor training programs;

   auditory training programs;

   and visual perceptual training programs.

6. Staff participation — teacher aide, classroom teachers, tutors, speech therapist.

- *Recreational Goals and Objectives*

   1. recreational skill development with emphasis on individual interest and choice
   2. exposure to and development of skills in a variety of leisure time pursuits
   3. development of physical skill and physical fitness

This is the time of life in which individuals certainly need support in developing a positive self-concept and improved self-esteem. Feelings of self-worth may be enhanced by increasing the students' abilities in a variety of areas. This can be done by teaching new skills and assisting students in developing new interests. It is also a time when students are very competitive in recreational events and it is a time when they can be supported and assisted in participating in (fair) competition. In addition to this, a variety of recreational and leisure time pursuits allow for increased social skills and an opportunity for students with proficiencies in one area to teach skills to others who have not yet learned these skills. Recreation gives further opportunity for a sense of accomplishment for development of self-sufficiency and, through many of the activities, improved physical health.

Programs and Activities Utilized to Meet These Objectives

1. Recreational Pursuits

   Swimming program

   Skating program

   Hiking

2. Leisure Time Pursuits

   Project Oriented Arts and Crafts

   Music — mainstreamed plus special events and special interest activities

3. Physical Development

   Students receive extra time with the physical education instructor, outside their mainstreamed classes

   The Dubnoff Program, Vanguard Program, Fernald technique, pencil grips, printing, writing

   Visualization and relaxation exercises, recreational activities

4. Camp Recskill — A summer camp for those students 10 years of age and younger.

   Integrated activities — gymnastics after school program, hockey, biking, intramurals (basketball, volleyball, floor hockey), summer swimming program

- *Prevocational Goals and Objectives*

  - To develop the values of work including economic, personal, and societal.

    a. recognition of occupational awareness and personal abilities

    b. community based study of work

    c. emphasis on good work habits and self-evaluation of products

    d. introduction of "in-school" work jobs and "home" responsibilities

This is an important area for this age student since many of them, at the end of this period of time, will be making decisions to move into vocationally oriented programs rather than academically oriented programs. General areas covered are the study of money, development of social skills, improved self-esteem, grooming, and punctuality. Although these are worth developing in themselves, they certainly are necessary in order to obtain and keep a job in later life. It is important during this period of time to develop vocationally related academic skills to maintain and improve good work habits and an awareness of traits necessary in all jobs. It is also a time that an infusion of career information into the curriculum is very often appropriate to make the necessary linkings between the curriculum being studied and its application in the world of work. Through social studies and discussions, it is a time to develop an understanding of industry, business, a variety of jobs in the community, and the training necessary for specific occupations.

Activities Utilized to Meet These Objectives

Career infusion: structured exercise — select jobs from job cluster, describe job conduct, do research on the job, give oral report, discuss report and arrange to go out to see work site, and discuss results. The resources would be those identified by students. Everyone will be able to participate with regard to ability.

Use of newspaper (reading related) to study career opportunities for older students.

In-school work jobs: cleaning, working in cafeteria, classroom maintenance, photocopying, assist with highest needs children, collating, sorting, assembly work (e.g., the school newspaper).

Safety lessons related to job selection (above).

Vocationally related academic skills — time, money handling, units of measurement, learn job related words and language, use of telephone.

- *Social and Emotional Goals and Objectives*
  - To create in students a better understanding of self and others
    a. expressing feelings and understanding one's own social strengths and weaknesses
    b. becoming aware of community support systems
    c. coping with emerging sexuality
    d. learning acceptance of responsibility for one's own actions

At this age, students are bridging the gap from childhood to adolescence. They must learn to deal appropriately with people from many groups including younger children, peers, and adults in the school and community. Students whose age places them at the upper end of this grouping must be ready to make the transition from placement in an elementary school to placement in a secondary school. Much of the success of this transition will be dependent on age-appropriate behavior. More specifically, they must be able to mix with various groups of people in social settings, to be considerate of others, and to learn to live within the rules of society. In addition to this, students will learn to be more independent when dealing with daily problems and to learn socially acceptable ways of expressing their feelings. They must learn to be ready to do their part in group projects so that they will be accepted by the group, thus improving self-concept. They must learn to be assertive when they think they are being misused. They must also learn about support systems within the community and the appropriate individuals and agencies to seek out for specific types of problems.

Activities Utilized to Meet These Objectives

- Interaction with existing programs such as recreational programs, school lunch programs, class trips, etc.

- Sex education, done through films, books, and discussions.

- Discussions of problems facing youth.

- Drug abuse, parents with emotional and/or alcohol problems, family life.

- Decision making, peer pressure and relationships.

- Using newspapers and magazines to illustrate and elaborate on the above mentioned topics.

- Speakers from outside agencies.

- Trips to various agencies in the community.

- Behavior management techniques to enhance socially acceptable behavior.

- Use of humor in the classroom.

- Provide positive feedback in the classroom for appropriate behaviors and responses.

- Provide opportunities for cooperative play to develop socially appropriate reactions.

- Teach appropriate responses to inappropriate verbal and physical interactions "Streetwise Program."

Life Skills Goals and Objectives

1. to increase logical thinking in decision making and practical applications of logical decision making

2. to increase personal management of self and environment

Many of the things involved in other parts of the curriculum can be classified as life skills; however, important things can be overlooked unless they are specified to be taught within a program. Following are general areas that should be built into a program for this age student.

- Improvement of the basic hygiene skills of all students.

- Promotion of self-help skills such as cleaning, laundry, understanding of purchasing power, proper eating habits and weight control, independence and mobility around the community, safety around the home, contributions to family life, including cleaning, cooking and assisting other members of the family with household chores.

- An understanding and appreciation of the variety of services that are available to them.

Activities Utilized to Meet These Objectives

- Daily check, private routine check with teacher if formal encouragement is needed.

- Self-help skills

  1. Cleaning — mop floor, clean tub, clean mirrors in life skills room (daily job) for those students who are less integrated.

  2. Laundry — on duty roster — fold, mend, sew buttons, use washer, dryer.

  3. Purchase power — play store, buy necessary life skills supplies.

  4. Eating habits — food groups work, good food versus junk food, monitor daily intake for examination.

  5. Walk to post office, skating rink, pharmacy, clinic, police station, grocery store.

  6. Domestic safety — understand label precautions and recognize danger.

  7. Wash dishes, set table, fold clothes, make bed (home program and school program).

  8. Grooming — selection of appropriate clothes, washing clothes, care of nails, teeth.

  9. Cook — soup, make salad, make sandwich, cook hamburger, fry an egg (or boil).

  10. Special projects to benefit total school.

- Community services projects

  1. Essential phone services — FIRE, POLICE.

  2. Other — Doctor's office, dentist's office, Public Health, Social Services, etc.

Fourteen Years of Age and Older (High Needs Students)

- *Academic Goals and Objectives*

1. improved functional communication skills (reading, listening, writing, and speaking)

2. improved functional mathematics skills (time, money, and measurement)

3. focus special studies based on interests and ability of individual students

It is during this age and time period for high needs students that the goals and objectives must shift from academics to the application of academic skills to life situations; for example, in language arts, the maintenance of reading skills and emphasis on practical comprehension skills. For those students who have been unable to learn basic reading skills, we must work on the development of functional reading and functional writing. Because of its occupational and social implications, great emphasis must be placed on the improvement of listening skills and following directions. In mathematics, operations and problem solving must be stressed involving common everyday problems, banking, and tax procedures. In doing this, a calculator should be used and an emphasis placed on time, measurement, and money to relate to occupational objectives, and consumer skills. Social studies and science are done on an individualized basis and through group discussions, very often utilizing newspapers in studying local and world geography, social problems, current events, and social and technological change.

Programs and Activities Utilized to Meet These Objectives

Language Arts

In general, the language arts program should produce changes in pupil behavior in most of the following ways:

1. changes in things known — content knowledge.

2. changes in things done — oral, written, and reading skills.

3. changes in things felt — attitudes.

4. changes in things valued — appreciation.

5. changes in things comprehended — understanding.

6. changes in judgment — capacity to form sensible conclusions about issues and people.

Listening and Speaking Objectives

1. To provide ample opportunity for students to practice the art of leadership through assignment of specific responsibilities.

2. To help a student develop the habit of listening carefully and intently, and the habit of asking or saying clearly and as courteously as possible what he needs to know so that he may do reasonably well what he needs to do. A student must realize that good listening

and speaking habits will add immeasurably to his success and happiness.

Experiences such as games, trips, T.V. programs, making purchases, introducing visitors, thanking them for contributions, role playing, interviewing, and telephone conversations are used.

Teacher Aides

1. tape recorder — compressed speech
2. films and filmstrips
3. television
4. telephone set
5. reading references

Writing

1. The primary objective is to train students to do the kind of writing which they may be called upon to do after they leave school:

   a. letter writing — social and business.

   b. filling out forms and reports.

2. Emphasis is on training the students to state clearly and simply what they wish to say. Quality rather than quantity is stressed.

3. Emphasis on spelling is continued.

Writing Skills Stressed

1. Review of sentence
2. Punctuation
3. Writing letters
4. Addressing envelopes
5. Developing written skills with the newspaper; e.g., answering advertisements
6. Dictionary skills

   a. alphabetical order

   b. spelling and pluralization

7. Developing vocabulary

   a. alternatives for overworked words

   b. development and usage of vocational vocabulary

   c. drills in corrective English; e.g., commonly misused word pairs (well, good, teach, learn)

Reading Program

1. To teach reading skills to the student.
2. To give practice in the application of the reading skills in practical and meaningful ways.

Skills Stressed

1. Identify words by means of:
   a. context clues
   b. root words
   c. homonyms
   d. prefixes
   e. suffixes
2. Understand the role of intonation.
3. Skim for specific information.
4. Follow sequence of cause and effect relationships.
5. Follow directions in materials.
6. Locate information.

Mathematics

1. To develop the ability to apply mathematical information, concepts, principles, and skills in various aspects of social and vocational life.
2. To assist the student to see a meaningful relationship between abstract mathematical knowledge and life experiences.
3. To develop competence in problem solving.

Topics: Basic Skills and Computation

1. Automobiles
   a. Buying/selling
   b. Costs of owning an automobile
2. Earnings
3. Household — measurement
4. Clothing — cost, measurement
5. Welfare — family allowances, pension plans
6. Budget
7. Personal loans
8. Insurance
9. Services
   a. Electricity and gas

   b. Telephone

   c. Postal service

Science: Objectives

   1. To develop an awareness of the environment and an understanding of scientific principles which govern the natural and physical world, and to develop the abilities to apply these principles to situations in everyday life.

   2. To develop the habits of careful and accurate observations and to encourage logical thinking.

   3. To train students to solve problems in a neat and careful manner so that others can comprehend their findings.

   4. To create an interest in as many fields of science as possible.

   5. To realize that an understanding of science contributes to the success of our daily lives.

   6. To improve study skills.

Topics

   1. Science and the Development of Man

   2. Air Pressure and Its Uses

   3. The Laws of Fluids

   4. The Nature and Control of Heat

   5. Climate, Weather, and Forecasting

   6. Exploring Our Solar System

   7. Man's Progress in Sending Messages

Social Studies

   1. Objectives — Occupational

      a. To assist students to realize the interrelationships existing between occupations and geographical and historical factors.

      b. To develop in students an understanding of how and why certain occupations disappear or are created in a community.

      c. To develop in students an interest in the variety of occupations in a community.

2. Objectives — Trade Unions

   a. To develop an understanding and appreciation of the role of labor unions.

   b. To develop an understanding and appreciation of the role of labor unions in relation to the individual.

   c. To develop an understanding of the nature and function of a union.

3. Objectives — Industry Unit

   a. To assist students to realize the interrelationships existing between industry and geographical and historical facts.

   b. To develop in students an understanding and appreciation of how and why some industries are feasible and practical in his/her local community and why some industries may tend to be unstable and vanish from the community.

   c. To develop in students an interest in the various industries that provide the economic base of his/her local community.

4. Objectives — International Organizations

   a. To make the students aware of international organizations; e.g., some organizations are formed for the purpose of defense, some for economic reasons, others for the purpose of assisting underdeveloped countries.

   b. To help students develop an understanding of their nation's role in these organizations. It is hoped that this will develop within the student a sense of brotherhood and tolerance for the people of other lands.

5. Objectives — National Problems Unit

   a. To develop in students a greater understanding and insight into the environment and the people who live in it.

   b. To develop in students an understanding and acceptance of others and their ways.

   c. To give students skills which will enable them to deal with many of the problems that constantly arise in our national lives.

6. Objectives — Civics

   a. To develop within the student an understanding of our various levels of government.

    b. To develop an understanding of and an interest in elections.

    c. To develop an understanding of the reasons why every citizen is morally obligated to vote in every election.

● *Recreational Goals and Objectives*

1. Promotion of physical fitness

2. Productive and worthy use of leisure time

3. Exposure to a variety of leisure time activities

4. Logical decision making regarding leisure time activities

This is certainly an important area for students of this age. Helping them make decisions regarding wise use of leisure time can assist them in many social, economic, and personal areas of life in the community. They must learn an appreciation for the wide diversity of leisure choices and life styles. They must explore and participate in these to assist in later life decision making. Development of specific skills must be stressed in school activities so that they may participate in the mainstream of leisure time activities throughout the school. This will certainly make vast contributions to their self-esteem and to their physical and intellectual development.

Programs and Activities Utilized to Meet These Objectives

1. Recreation and education; i.e., camping and self-maintenance.

2. Participation in school dances, winter carnival.

3. Viewing current movies.

4. Roller skating, bowling.

5. Swimming.

6. Arts and Crafts — many students can offer their expertise; i.e., making Christmas decorations, fly-tying (salmon and trout flies) and exposure to community artisans.

7. Team sports — school teams, intramurals, Special Olympics (where appropriate) and community based teams.

8. Music programs.

9. Games.

10. Planning and organizing a variety of special events; i.e., during specific holidays.

- *Prevocational and Vocational Goals and Objectives*

    1. Self-awareness and acceptance of personal strengths and weaknesses

    2. Realistic expectations of occupational requirements

    3. Exposure to real life job experiences

    4. Infusion of career information with class discussions

    5. Placement of individual students in specialized training programs or employment

This is extremely critical with students of this age, as this is the time when students come in the secondary school setting and must work through a process of preparing themselves to enter either a traditional training program or the work force. Each student's program must be individualized as he or she moves through this process because of his or her own strengths, weaknesses, and interests. During this period of time, students must be reflective and gain better self-understanding as it relates to the world of work in general. They must also develop an understanding of the relationship between academic knowledge and work. They must realize that there are many attributes to bring to an employer, that the ability to do the job is not necessarily the reason for gaining the job or being able to keep one. They must learn about social and personal skills necessary to be successful in the world of work.

Programs and Activities Utilized to Meet These Objectives

A total work readiness outline is listed which has been gleaned from a variety of programs such as the Janus Educational Design Materials, Turner Career Guidance Materials, media materials, Career Caravan Materials, Hampton Publications, as well as teacher-designed materials and community resources.

Listed below is a sample three-unit program utilized to meet prevocational and vocational goals and objectives:

1. Value of work:

    verbalizes personal, societal, economic values of work.

    expresses positive attitude toward work.

2. Occupational self-awareness:

    identifies own occupational interests.

    identifies own occupational needs, wants, preferences.

    identifies own occupational skills.

identifies own occupational aptitudes.

identifies own occupational values.

3. Job awareness:

   classifies jobs into groups or clusters.

   identifies general conditions of various jobs.

   identifies skills needed for various jobs.

   identifies training needed for various jobs.

   identifies job opportunities available locally.

   identifies sources of job information.

4. Job seeking:

   can use classified ads (or gets help).

   aware of local employment agency (Manpower).

   aware of signs/announcement regarding jobs.

   aware of using personal contacts to find jobs.

5. Job Application:

   prepares a résumé (or gets help).

   writes letters of application (or gets help).

   completes job application form (or presents prepared form).

   conducts self appropriately in interview — appropriate dress, arrives on time, answers questions simply and honestly, asks appropriate questions, maintains eye contact, good posture, firm handshake, introduces self and calls interviewer by name.

6. Job Maintenance:

   aware of good work habits — honesty, following directions, working with others, willingness to work, satisfactory rate, accepts supervision, accepts criticism.

   aware of importance of punctuality, good attendance.

   aware of importance of high quality performance on job.

   aware of importance of good interpersonal relationships with supervisor and coworkers.

   aware of importance of adjusting to working conditions.

   aware of importance of appropriate dress on the job.

   understands good safety habits.

aware of rights of workers.

aware of appropriate procedure for changing jobs.

There should also be a work experience program in the community.

- *Social and Emotional Goals and Objectives*

    1. Healthy attitudes and values regarding human sexuality

    2. Socially acceptable behavior

    3. Dealing affectively with human emotions of self and others

    4. Learning to utilize community support systems

Children, during adolescence, are becoming more aware of other individuals in their environment and are becoming less egocentric. The classroom, of course, is a social situation where they can learn many social skills. Reinforcement of these skills will enable them to improve their relationships with other individuals. They must learn to respect the feelings of others, property, and ideas. They must also recognize their own strengths and weaknesses as well as those of others and to accept them. They must learn to accept rules and if they disagree with rules, they must learn the proper routes to take in order to have these rules discussed and modified. Learning in this area is often incidental and arises out of curriculum content and classroom situations.

Programs and Activities Utilized to Meet These Objectives

1. Role playing is a major technique for dealing with many topics in the social and emotional areas

2. Survival, a guide to living on your own, deals with: individuality, handling stress, communication with others, maintaining relationships, and presenting your point of view

3. The Getting Along Series of Skills

4. After School Is Out

5. Life Skills: Me and Others

6. Life Skills: Attitudes in Everyday Living

7. I Can Say No

8. Feeling Good About Yourself Books and Cards

9. Guest speakers dealing with a variety of topics such as drug awareness, human sexuality, brainstorming and group problem solving

- *Life Skills Goals and Objectives*

  1. Students can demonstrate wise decision making skills.

  2. Students can demonstrate effectiveness in real life situations.

  3. Students can demonstrate ability for management of themselves and their environment.

It is difficult to separate life skills from the previously mentioned goals and objectives formally covered in this document, at this age level. It is obviously interrelated with academics, recreation, social and emotional development, and occupational readiness. This section, therefore, will deal with a variety of life skills not directly related to the other sections. Specific emphasis must be made on problem solving skills, human relations, and independent living skills.

Programs and Activities That Are Utilized to Meet These Objectives

  1. Trips, both day and overnight trips of a variety where planning for the trips must be done by the students.

  2. Family life program dealing with relationships within the family as well as with human sexuality and child rearing.

  3. Bachelor living which gives boys hands-on experience in cooking, sewing, shopping, and child care.

  4. First aid and safety programs.

  5. Turner Livingstone reading series.

  6. Hampton publications materials.

  7. Educational Design Inc. materials.

  8. Janus materials.

  9. Community awareness — including transportation, shopping, leisure time activities, budgeting and home management.

  10. Dealing with problems:

      recognizing problems;

      defining problems;

      choosing solutions to problems.

UTILIZING THE GOALS AND OBJECTIVES FORMAT

Designing programs based on goals and objectives seems to be equally important to parents and teachers and has many benefits. Teachers responsible for part-time special classes can monitor their progress toward integration into regular classes by:

- Designing reports that state the number of periods per week each student is in Special Education classes.

- Offering to assist regular classroom teachers with appropriate materials to meet the needs of the student.

- Assisting regular classroom teachers in assessment of Special Education students.

- Counseling with parents to ensure that they understand the reporting system for Special Education students.

- Increasing the amount of time a Special Education student spends in a regular class as compared with the amount of time he/she spends in a special class.

- Consulting with regular classroom teachers regarding strategies for use with students and their individual learning styles.

In rural areas with traditionally conservative backgrounds, teaching human sexuality in the school system is always a controversial issue, especially for school board members who must be either reappointed or reelected periodically. Board members and senior administrative staff who attended the joint meetings with parents and professionals in discussing goals and objectives, were amazed at the unanimity at which parents wanted schools to take a major role in teaching their children about human sexuality. Parents felt that the teachers had access to properly designed materials and in working with similar age group of students, could best assist their children in dealing with their own sexuality and appropriate behaviors. As a result of these parent requests, the professional staff from Planned Parenthood was contacted and they developed an age-appropriate curriculum for special needs students and assisted teachers in piloting this program with their classes.

VERGE HOUSE PROGRAM

The Verge House program, for 18- to 21-year-old highest needs students, is often referred to as being new and unique. In today's educational systems, it is certainly a unique program. However, many individuals are amazed that it was actually one of the very first models designed to assist the mentally handicapped of North America. During the period from 1850 to 1880, pioneers such as Seguin, Howe, Wilbur, and others, believed that through education and training, the mentally handicapped could be able to live more normal lives in society. The first institutions created by these pioneers were small, homelike, and located in the heart of the community. A careful study of the records show that these institutions were remarkably successful in achieving their stated purpose. For example, by 1869, eighteen years after Howe had founded the Massachusetts School for the Feeble Minded Youth, its total enrollment was still less than 90. During that period, 465 children had been admitted, 365 had been discharged — many of them as self-supporting members of the community.

It was only after this period, starting in about 1870, that emphasis shifted to sheltering the mentally handicapped from society and society from the mentally handicapped. However, the word shelter basically meant to isolate. It was during this period that pity changed into fear and scorn and mental retardation began to be considered a menace. Laws were passed forbidding marriage and permitting or mandating sterilization and the permanent segregation of the feeble minded.

Perhaps this is the one area of education where we really must get "back to basics" and utilize those ideas that were formally successful, namely that communities must show love and acceptance and take responsibility for their mentally handicapped citizens.

Certainly the process of discussing and reaching consensus on goals and objectives for special class students can lead to new and creative programs designed to meet these goals and objectives. The curriculums developed often take a fresh look at old problems and more importantly, are designed to utilize local and community resources in their application.

CHAPTER 6 REFERENCE MATERIALS

Multidimensional Curriculum Guides

Anderson, Val, and Smart, David, *Primary Learning Skills Program*, Benefic Press, Chicago, 1980.

Address: Benefic Press
1900 N. Narragansett
Chicago, IL 60639

Dallas County Mental Health/Mental Retardation Center; Walling, Jean; Baugh, Carol; Moss, Barbara; Ort, Elizabeth, (ed.), *Radea: Testing and Remediation*, 1976.

Dallas County Mental Health/Mental Retardation Center and Moss, Barbara, *SAIL: Skills to Achieve Independent Living*, 1979.

Address: Melton Peninsula Inc.
1949 Stemmons Freeway, Suite 690
Dallas, TX 75207

Hannah, Marta; Millhouse, John; Sauvageot, Audrey; Froelick, Arlene; Zidar, Phyllis; Spinks, Nancy; and Landau, Paula, *SCIL: Systematic Curriculum for Independent Living*, 1977.

Address: Academic Therapy Publications
20 Commercial Blvd.
Novato, CA 94947

Linkenhoker, Dan, and McCarron, Lawrence, *Street Survival Skills Questionnaire*, Common Market Press, Dallas, TX, 1983.

Address: Common Market Press
P. O. Box 45628
Dallas, TX 78245

Merkley, Elaine, *Becoming a Learner*, Charles E. Merrill, Co., Columbus, OH, 1972.

Address: Charles E. Merrill Co.
Columbus, OH 43216

Specific Goal Area Curriculum Guides and Kits

Agard, Judith; McCullough, Nancy; and Santangelo-Broderson, Lynda, *Marathon: A Program for Teaching Social Behaviors Needed for Work and Community Living*, 1983.

Address: Stanfield Film Associates
P. O. Box 1983-90406
Santa Monica, CA

Blau, Melinda, *Following Written Directions, Canadian Reading Skills Series*, 1979.

Address: Edu-Media Holdings, Ltd.
Kitchener, Ontario

Coronet Reading Program.

Address: Coronet, the Multimedia Co.
65 E. South Water St.
Chicago, IL 60601

Dinkmeyer, D., and Dinkmeyer D. Jr., *Developing Understanding of Self and Others*.
Address: American Guidance Services
Circle Pines, MN 55014-1796

Dubnoff Programs-Teaching Resources Inc.

Address: 50 Pond Park Road
Hingham, MA 02043

Dupont, Henry; Gardner, O.S.; and Brody, David, *Toward Affective Development*, American Guidance Services, Circle Pines, MN, 1984.

Address: AGS American Guidance Services
Circle Pines, MN 55014-1796

Fearon-Pitman Publishers, *The Job Box: Pacemaker Vocational Resource Module*, 1978.

Address: Fearon-Pitman Publishers
             6 Davis Drive
             Belmont, CA 94002

Frost, Jack, and Ratliff, Linda, *Workers We Know*, Chronicle Guidance Publications Inc., 1973.

Address: Moravia, NY 13118

Gallogley, Gloria, et.al., *Growing Up* (Life Skills Kit), Novalis Publishing Co., Ottawa, Ontario, 1984.

Address: P. O. Box 9700 Terminal
             Ottawa, Ontario
             K1G 4B4

Goldbert, H.R., and Greenberger, Bernard, *The Job Ahead: A Career Reading Series (4)*, Science Research Associates, Chicago, 1977.

Hill, Sylvia (ed.), *SRA Schoolhouse Comprehension Patterns*, Science Research Associates, Chicago, 1974.

Address: 155 N. Wacker Drive
             Chicago, IL 60606

Janus Career — Education Materials (Series).

Address: Janus Book Publishers
             2501 Industrial Parkway West
             Hayward, CA 94545

Math Facts, Milton Bradley Co.

Address: 443 Shaker Rd.
             East Longmeadow, MA 01028

Pathways in Science, Globe Book Co., New York, 1968.

Address: 50 West 23 Street
             New York, NY 10010

Quinn, Treva, *Mafex Math Survival Series*, 1969-Revised 1980.
Address: Mafex Associates, Inc.
             90 Cherry St. Box 519
             Johnstown, PA 15907

Raths, Louis; Wasserman, Selma; and Wasserman, Jack, *Thinking Skills Development Program*, Benefic Press, Chicago, IL, 1982.

Address: Benefic Press
             1900 N. Narragansett
             Chicago, IL 60639

Richardson, Hazel A., *Games for Junior and Senior High Schools*, Burgess Publishing Co., Minneapolis, MN, 1957.

Address: Burgess Publishing Co.
            7108 Ohms Lane
            Minneapolis, MN 55435

Sanford, Adrian, et.al., *Audio Reading Kit*, Educational Progress, A division of the Educational Development Corporation, 1976.

Address: P. O. Box 45663
            Tulsa, OK 74145

Social Learning Curriculum

Address: Charles E. Merrill Publishing Co.
            1300 Alum Cr. Drive
            Columbus, OH 43216

Taylor, Edward, and Hamilton, Garry, *On the Job: Now Is Tomorrow Series*, The Book Society of Canada, Ltd., Agincourt, Ontario, Canada, 1979.

Taylor, Ellen, and Stewart, Charles, *Practicing Occupational Reading Skills* (a series), Random House, New York, 1982.

Address: 301 E. 50th St.
            New York, NY 10022

Turner, Richard H., *Turner Career Guidance Series*, Follett Publishing Co., Chicago, 1974.

Address: 1010 W. Washington Blvd.
            Chicago, IL 60607

Wood, John D., *Using Money Series*, Frank E. Richard Publishing Co., Liverpool, NY, 1982.

Address: Frank E. Richard Publishing Co.
            P. O. Box 370
            Liverpool, NY 10388

Multilevel Series and Kits

Allmond, Phyllis, and Moch, Valerie, *Pacemaker Arithmetic Program*, Fearon-Pitman Publishers, Inc., Belmont, Ca, 1974.

Address: Fearon-Pitman Publishers, Inc.
            6 Davis Drive
            Belmont, CA 94002

Anderson, Donald G., *New Practice Readers* (Series), Webster Division, McGraw-Hill Book Co, New York, 1978.

Address: 1221 Ave. of the Americas
            New York, NY 10017

Big Books, 1983.

Address: The Wright Group Publications
            7620 Miramar Road, Suite 41001
            San Diego, CA 92126

Distar (Language, Reading, and Math Multilevel Kits).

Address: Science Research Associates
155 North Wacker Drive
Chicago, IL 60606

Dolch Materials.

Address: Lakeshore Equipment Co.
6036 Claremont Ave.
Oakland, CA 94618

Gagné Robert, *Skill Modes in Mathematics* (Kits levels 1, 2, and 3), Science Research Associates, Chicago, 1974.

Address: 155 North Wacker Drive
Chicago, IL 60606

Greenberg, Mal (ed.), *Basic Skills Program Reading*, King Features, 1977.

Address: LSR Learning Associates, Inc.
278 Haypath Rd.
Old Bethpage, NY

High Noon Books (High Age Interest-Low Vocabulary).

Address: Ann Arbor Publishers
P. O. Box 7249
Naples, FL 33941

Laubach, Frank C., and Kirk, Elizabeth M., *Laubach Reading Program*, New Readers Press, Syracuse, NY, 1968.

Address: New Readers Press
Box 131
Syracuse, NY 13210

Laubach, Frank C., and Kirk, Elizabeth M., *Laubach Way to Reading*, Laubach Literacy, Syracuse, NY, 1981.

Address: Publishing Division of Laubach Literacy International
Box 131
Syracuse, NY 13210

Liddle, Wm. (ed.), *Reading for Concepts* (Series), Webster Division, McGraw-Hill Book Co., New York, 1977.

Address: 1221 Ave. of the Americas
New York, NY 10020

Martin, William, *Instant Readers*, Holt, Rinehart & Winston, New York, 1970 (Book-tape series).

Address: 383 Madison Ave.
New York, NY 10020

Multiple Skills Series Programs for Individualized Instruction.

Address: Richard A. Boning
             Barnell Loft
             958 Church St.
             Baldwin, NY 11510

Peabody Language Development Kits (various levels).

Address: American Guidance Service Inc.
             Publishers Building
             Circle Pines, MN 55014

Readers Digest Skill Builders (Pegasus Edition).

Address: Readers Digest Assoc. of Canada, Educational Division
             215 Redfern Ave.
             Montreal, P.Q.
             H3Z 2V9

Specific Skills Series, Barnell Loft, Ltd.

Address: 958 Church Street
             Baldwin, NY 11510

SRA Reading Laboratory (Several levels of kits), Science Research Associates, Chicago.

Address: 155 N. Wacker Dr.
             Chicago, IL 60606

Sullivan Programmed Reading Series, Webster Division, McGraw-Hill Book Co., 1973.

Sullivan, M.D., and Howlett, James S., *Programmed Math* (series), Webster Division, McGraw-Hill Book Co., New York, 1975.

Address: 1221 Ave. of the Americas
             New York, NY 10020

Suppliers of a Variety of Developmental Materials

DLM Learning Materials.

Address: 7440 Natchez Ave.
             Niles, IL 60648

Educational Insights.

Address: 20435 South Tillman Avenue
             Carson, CA 90746

Instructo Materials.

Address: Instructo Products Co.
             Cedar Hollow Rd.
             Paoli, PA 19301

Manolakes, George, et.al., *Try, Experiences for Young Children*, Noble & Noble Publishers Inc., 1967.

Address: 1 Dag Hammerskjold Plaza
New York, NY 10017

Scholar's Choice Materials, Scholar's Choice Ltd., 1963.

Address: 50 Ballantyne Ave.
Stratford, Ontario
N5A 6T9

Individual Books and Programs

Ainsworth, Barbara; Trautman, David; and Layton, James, *Reading Labels and Signs*, Hampden Publications, Baltimore, MD, 1979.

Address: Hampden Publications, Inc.
Box 4873
Baltimore, MD

Baratta-Lorton, Mary, *Mathematics Their Way*, Addison-Wesley Publishing Co., Reading, Mass., 1976.

Address: South Street
Reading, MA 01867

Blum, Gloria, and Blum, Barry, *Feeling Good Cards (1981)*, *Feeling Good About Yourself: A Guide for Working with People Who Have Disabilities (1981)*, The Sound Filmstrip, *I Can Say No*.

Address: Feeling Good Associates
507 Palma Way
Mill Valley, CA 94941

Burt and Brower, *Education for Sexuality: Concepts and Programs for Teaching*, W.B. Saunders Co., Philadelphia, 1970.

Address: West Washington Square
Philadelphia, PA 19105

Canfield, Jack, and Wells, Harold C., *100 Ways to Enhance Self-Concept in the Classroom*, Prentice-Hall Inc., Englewood Cliffs, NJ, 1976.

Address: Prentice-Hall, Inc.
Englewood Cliffs, NJ 07632

Carlaw R., and Raithby, P., *Applying Mathematics*, McGraw-Hill Book Co., New York, 1967.

Address: 1221 Ave. of the Americas
New York, NY 10020

Deiner, Penny Lou, *Resources for Teaching Young Children with Special Needs*, Harcourt Brace Jovanovich, San Diego, CA, 1983.

Address: Harcourt Brace Jovanovich
1250 Sixth Avenue
San Diego, CA 92101

Donlon, Edward, and Burton, Louise, *The Severely and Profoundly Handicapped, A Practical Approach to Teaching*, 1976, Grune & Stratton, a subsidiary of Harcourt Brace Jovanovich, 1976.

Address: 1250 Sixth Avenue
             San Diego, CA 92101

Elrich, Thomas F., *Forms in Your Life*, Modern Curriculum Press, Cleveland, OH, 1981.
Address: 13900 Prospect Rd.
             Cleveland, OH 44136

Farrow, Elvira, and Hill, Carol, *Montessori on a Limited Budget*, Montessori Workshop, Ithaca, NY, 1975.
Address: Montessori Workshop
             501 Salem Dr.
             Ithaca, NY 14850

Fernald, G., *Remedial Techniques in Basic Subjects*, McGraw-Hill Book Co., New York, 1943.
Address: McGraw-Hill Book Co.
             1221 Ave. of the Americas
             New York, NY 10020

Glassman, Martyn, and Kisiow, Elaine, *Cooperation and Community Life*, Cooperation College of Canada, 1983.
Address: 141 105th St. West
             Saskatoon, Saskatchewan
             S7N 1N3

Glatthorn, Allan, and Christensen, Jane, *Patterns of Communicating*, D.C. Heath & Co., 1973.
Address: 125 Spring St.
             Lexington, MA 02173

Goodman, Kenneth, and Goodman, Yetta, *Linguistics, Psycholinguistics and the Teaching of Reading*, International Reading Association, 1980.
Address: 801 Barksdale Rd.
             P. O. Box 8139
             Newark, DE 19714-8139

Gordon, Sol, *The Teenage Survival Book*, Harper and Row, Scranton, PA, 1981.
Address: Keystone Industrial Park
             Scranton, PA 18512

Gossage, Loyce, and Briggs, Milton, *Mathematics Skill Builder*, South-Western Publishing Co., Cincinnati, OH, 1969.
Address: 5101 Madison Rd.
             Cincinnati, OH 45227

Hayden, Margaret, et. al., *Mathematics for Daily Use*, Doubleday, New York, 1980.
Address: 245 Park Ave.
             New York, NY 10017

Hehner, Barbara (ed.), *Blissymbolics for Use*, Blissymbolics Communication Institute, Toronto, Ontario, 1980.

Address: Blissymbolics Communication Institute
350 Rumsey Road
Toronto, Ontario
M4G 1R8

Instant Language Builders, 1985.

Address: Methuen Publications
2330 Midland Ave.
Agincourt, Ontario
M1S 1P7

Levin, Beatrice J., *Real Life Reading: A Scholastic Program in Functional Reading*, Scholastic Book Services, 1980.

Address: 1290 Wall Street West
Lyndhurst, NJ 07071

Nelson, L. D., and Liedtke, W., *Mathematical Experiences in Early Childhood*, Encyclopedia Britannica Publications, Chicago, IL, 1982.

Address: 310 Michigan Ave.
Chicago, IL 60604

Nelson, Leslie and Lorbeer, George, *Science Activities for Elementary Children*, Wm. C. Brown & Co., Dubuque, Iowa, 1976.

Address: 2460 Kerper Blvd.
Dubuque, IA 52001

Perceive and Respond, Modern Education Corporation.

Address: P. O. Box 721
Tulsa, OK 74101

Wittels, Harriet, and Greisman, John, *How to Spell It: A Dictionary of Commonly Misspelled Words*, Grosset & Dunlap, New York, 1973. (Originally published as *The Perfect Speller*.)

Available from: Fitzhenry and Whiteside, Ltd.
195 Allstate Parkway
Markham, Ontario
L3R 4T8

Wood, Bob, *Environmental Science*, Holt, Rinehart & Winston of Canada Ltd., Toronto, 1975.

Address: Holt, Rinehart & Winston
383 Madison Ave.
New York, NY 10017

Woodruff, G.W.; Moore, G.N.; Nadig, N.S., *Spelling Words in Use*, Curriculum Associates, North Billerica, MA, 1974.

Address: Curriculum Associates
5 Esquire Rd.
North Billerica, MA 01862

CHAPTER 7

Evaluation

The perfection of any matter,
the highest or the lowest,
touches on the divine.

Martin Buber

Evaluation is an essential part of any system of service delivery and must include evaluation of personnel, individual programs, and the system as a whole. In recent years, accountability has become a catch word. True accountability in education should be judged on the goals achieved with students. Accountability, as usually translated by government departments and funding agencies, is simply a bookkeeping function. For example, accountability, as defined by a funding agency, would be to determine that the salary charged against Special Education funds is going to a teacher who is actually working in Special Education. True accountability would include not only that fact, but also that the teacher is positively affecting the students with whom he or she comes in contact.

EVALUATION OF STAFF

Evaluation of individual personnel must be conducted in an honest and positive manner to meet its prime goal, which is staff growth. Just as children need positive feedback, staff members need positive feedback as well. Large doses of negative criticism to staff members will do nothing but cause them to be extremely defensive. However, honest, negative criticism should be given along with accompanying positive suggestions for improving their work.

In addition to the supervision aspect of evaluation, evaluation of individual personnel should look at not only how they function on the job, but their training, interests, and other positions within the system in which they might be better suited than the position they presently hold. Sometimes a staff member who can function only marginally in one position might be extremely effective with a change of position. This might include a change of age level of students, a change in the functional level of students they work with, or a complete role change doing a different job within the system.

Evaluation of individual staff members cannot be looked at independently of the evaluation of the program in which they work. This is true because all of us have our own learning styles and preferred methods of operation. Only too often, even when we are aware of this, we tend to evaluate in terms of how we would do the job. In discussing staff evaluation, it is therefore critical to know who did the evaluation and how it was done. It is also extremely helpful to have a composite picture in evaluation of staff. That is, an evaluation report from principals and/or central office staff, a report as to measurable growth of students under this teacher's responsibility area, and a report of program satisfaction from parents. When judging personnel by a composite picture such as suggested, very often a totally different person seems to appear than does when simply reading a supervision report filled out by a superior.

PROGRAM EVALUATION

One excellent way of documenting program effectiveness is by use of ratio comparisons. Conventional research designs using control or matched groups is usually not useful in evaluating programs, since the mandate of the school is to offer service to children, not to be a research agency.

DEVELOPING RATIOS OF PROGRESS

Reporting of student gain by pre- and post-test measurements does not truly show the impact of the program because it does not relate this gain to the rate of the child's previous progress. This can be done by developing ratios of previous development prior to the time of assessment.

Ratios of progress can be used with reading, mathematics, perceptual development, or more global development in the case of preschool and more severely handicapped young children. Take the function being assessed and divide this by the expected (average) functional level; this will equal the developmental quotient at the time.

For example, if a student is reading at the grade 1.6 level but his expected reading level would be grade 3.6, then his developmental quotient is .44. When this child is placed in a program especially designed to assist him in this area, the effectiveness of this program is measured by taking a developmental gain and dividing this by the length of time that he has been involved in the program. If the same student we used as an example earlier were to be involved in a program which raised his reading level to the grade 2.3 level or a gain of nine months in reading when reassessed at the end of a one-year period, this would show a program effectiveness ratio of .75. Note: This may not be an appropriate form of evaluation for the lowest functioning students.

The advantage of this method is that the child's present progress can truly be compared with his past performance. In addition to this, the teachers and others involved in assisting the student get positive feedback regarding the role which they are playing in his/her educational program. This is especially important in the skill development years of elementary school, because children normally go from one teacher to a new teacher each year. Even though children may be making considerable progress, they are often viewed as the students performing the poorest in the new teacher's classroom because she/he does not have past performance versus present performance comparison.

In addition to the teachers receiving positive feedback, this is certainly helpful data to have when meeting with the student's parents to show them that, yes, he is making excellent progress relative to the progress he had made prior to being placed on an individualized program.

PARENT AND CLASSROOM TEACHER EVALUATION OF PROGRAMS

In addition to observational reports, and objective data reports, it is extremely helpful to understand how parents perceive the program and their child's progress. It is strongly suggested that for each type of program being offered within a school system that a questionnaire form be designed to measure parent satisfaction in each program. (See Figure 7-1.)

As previously discussed, in systems where the resource teacher is viewed as not only a resource to students but a resource to teachers, principals, and parents, there is additional opportunity to evaluate program effectiveness. This is done through the opinions of the classroom teachers, who in most cases, made the initial referral of students for assessment and programming. Many regular classroom teachers in the elementary school have several students on special or individualized programs; therefore, it is important that such a questionnaire be kept short and easy to complete for the classroom teacher.

Figure 7-2 is a sample of one such questionnaire which has been utilized to evaluate and strengthen program and staff. This information is helpful, not only in viewing the individual programs of students, but in how effectively the resource program is servicing individual schools within the system, and when totaled together, how effective the resource program is throughout the whole school system.

Not only is it important to have the classroom teacher's opinion regarding the program designed for each student in their care, but also it is equally

SPECIAL PROGRAM PARENT EVALUATION FORM

Child _____ Grade _____ Age _____

Teacher _____ School _____

Parents _____

_____

Please rate the following questions regarding your child and his/her program by circling a number from 1 to 5; 5 representing the most positive response and 1 representing the most negative response:

1. Your opinion regarding the appropriateness of the program designed for your child.

       1   2   3   4   5

2. Your opinion as to the practicality of the program designed for your use.

       1   2   3   4   5

3. To what degree have you been able to follow this program?

       1   2   3   4   5

4. To what degree do you feel that the teachers have followed the specific suggestions given to them?

       1   2   3   4   5

5. Your opinion as to your child's progress on this program.

       1   2   3   4   5

6. Comments

_____

_____

_____

_____

FIGURE 7-1

SPECIAL PROGRAM CLASSROOM TEACHER EVALUATION FORM

Student _____ Grade _____ Age _____

Teacher _____ School _____

Remedial time per week _____ Months on Program _____

Please rate the following questions regarding the above student and his/her program by circling a number from 1 to 5; 5 representing the most positive response and 1 representing the most negative response:

1. Your opinion regarding the appropriateness of the program designed for this student.

    1   2   3   4   5

2. Your opinion as to the practicality of the program designed for use by the classroom teacher.

    1   2   3   4   5

3. To what degree have you been able to follow this program?

    1   2   3   4   5

4. To what degree do you feel that the parents have followed the specific suggestions given to them?

    1   2   3   4   5

5. Your opinion as to the student's progress on this program.

    1   2   3   4   5

6. Do you believe that this student's program would progress faster if your school had volunteer tutors to assist classroom teachers with special programs?

    1   2   3   4   5

7. Comments

_____

_____

_____

_____

FIGURE 7-2

important to have the parents' opinion as to the appropriateness of the program designed for their child. In this way, parents feel that they have some input into the design and evaluation of their child's program and that their feelings are considered important as far as the school is concerned.

EVALUATING THE ENTIRE DELIVERY SYSTEM

Evaluation is necessary if programs are to be dynamic and continue to improve. The same is of course true in evaluation of the total system of service delivery in any school district.

There are several instruments available commercially to assist with evaluation of school systems, including a Special Education section published by the National Study of School Evaluation in the United States. It is the authors' opinion, however, that these commerical assessment instruments do not take a broad enough view of child-parent needs, nor do they look at the school as an integral and essential part of a community, but more as a separate system in isolation. Figure 7-3 is a list of fifteen criteria that can be used as a basis for evaluating the service delivery model offered by an individual school system.

This view of system evaluation is comprehensive, but is dependent upon how it is to be conducted. It can be utilized as an internal instrument for senior administrators to assess strengths and needs of their own system and to determine what additional programs may be required to make the system as comprehensive as possible.

A more helpful way of conducting this evaluation might be to utilize not only senior administrators but a committee willing to work on this project. The committee could be composed of representatives from the school board, administrative staff, school principals, regular classroom teachers, special education teachers, a cross section of parents, and other selected individuals from the community at large. The benefit of this representative committee evaluation procedure is that when strengths and needs are obvious they can be translated much more readily to other individuals in the community and also to funding agencies when it is necessary to establish new programs or to fill in gaps in services.

Special Education administrators might well consider one additional form of system evaluation — that is, to have other Special Education administrators visit and evaluate their system. It is most helpful if the individuals chosen for this task come from systems similar in several demographic ways. These individuals, prior to visitations, should be supplied with a model of the service delivery system, the goals and objectives within the system for each individual program, and information about the unique features of the school system being evaluated. Following that, they should be free to observe special education procedures, to meet with principals, regular classroom teachers, special education teachers, administrative staff, parents, and students. The evaluators should supply the school system with a report including their opinions on how effectively the school system is meeting its goals and objectives through

PARAMETERS IN SYSTEM EVALUATION

- Proper referral procedures

- Proper assessment procedures.

- Development of a variety of settings to deliver services according to the child's needs, ranging from special schools to adaptive materials in the regular classroom.

- Parental input into assessment, placement, and program.

- Early identification procedures:

  (1) screening;

  (2) liaison with preschool professionals in local community.

- Staff-student ratios appropriate for the needs of the children serviced.

- Proper utilization of teacher aides.

- Proper physical equipment and facilities.

- Proper and adequate curriculum materials.

- Individualized educational planning.

- Liaison with other helping professions within the community.

- Proper parent reporting procedures.

- Program evaluation:

  (1) individual student evaluation;

  (2) individual program evaluation.

- Parent appeal procedures.

- Student placement at the completion of school career:

  (1) additional training opportunities;

  (2) employment opportunities.

FIGURE 7-3

their special education service delivery model. In addition to this, they should report areas of strengths and weaknesses that they have observed and utilize their experience in making positive concrete suggestions for improvement of the system.

INDIVIDUAL STUDENT EVALUATION

The concept of evaluation must include individual student evaluation and the way in which this is reported to parents. Often it is the misunderstanding of reports which go home concerning students that can cause conflict between home and school. Report cards are notorious for being misunderstood or misinterpreted both by students and parents. Usually these misunderstandings can be resolved through person-to-person discussion of what the items really mean.

Parents of students having "special needs" can be even more confused because of the variety of reports which are sent home, and the tendency to use jargon in reports and meetings. It is suggested that students being assisted by individualized programs be continually evaluated in their program in the regular classroom, as well as the individualized portion of their program administered by the classroom teacher and tutor. These reports should deal with specific areas of development and skills being worked on with each individual student. Their progress on these skills should be shown on these forms and should be a consensus between the classroom teacher and the resource teacher.

Figures 7-4 and 7-5 are two sample forms designed by resource teachers for reporting to parents. One is utilized at the primary (kindergarten)–Grade 1 levels and the other is utilized at the Grades 2-6 levels. The form utilized at the primary (kindergarten)–Grade 1 levels is clear and concise and easily understood by parents. The form used at the Grades 2-6 levels should contain a page explaining the terms utilized. In addition to this, the form at the Grades 2-6 levels is extremely lengthy and often a student is being given assistance and individualized programming in only one or two areas contained on this report. In an attempt to simplify this reporting procedure, a program was devised for use on a microcomputer to print out only those sections of the report required for each individual student in an attempt to simplify and improve home-school communication.

EVALUATION OF MAINSTREAMED STUDENTS
BY REGULAR CLASSROOM TEACHERS

Evaluating special class students mainstreamed for part of their program into regular classrooms is a perplexing problem for educators. One of two extreme positions is often taken. The student is evaluated in the same manner as regular class students and is therefore doomed to failure. Even more frequently, these students have minimal expectations placed upon their performance and are routinely passed on from grade to grade. More

RESOURCE REPORT

Key

1. is working on

2. improvement shown

3. has completed

4. could benefit from
   extra help at home

5. little improvement,
   re-assessment required

P(K) - Gr. 1

Name _____

School _____ Grade _____

Date of Report _____

Times per Cycle _____

Setting: Individual (   ),   Small Group (   ),   Classroom (   )

Assessed by Speech Pathologist _____

	December	March	June
MATHEMATICS			
Counts orally 1 to ____			
Recognizes numbers 0 to ____			
Counts items correctly			
Makes sets to equal numbers			
Can add to ____			
Can subtract to ____			
Makes patterns or sequences ____			

Comments   _____

_____

_____

READING

	December	March	June
Recognizes letters			
Makes letters			
Reads books with someone (shared)			
Recognizes sight words in readers			
Language experience (tells stories, has them written down, retells them)			
Points to words in written text			

Comments _____

_____

_____

CONCEPT DEVELOPMENT

Recognizes colors			
Recognizes shapes			
Uses size words			
Uses position words (under, inside, etc.)			
Vocabulary development			
Speaking in sentences			
Can tell the differences between figures (shapes, numbers, letters)			

Comments _____

_____

_____

	December	March	June
PHYSICAL DEVELOPMENT			
Shows adequate movement skills			
Shows adequate fine motor skills (drawing, printing, cutting, etc.)			

Comments _____

_____

_____

SCHOOL-RELATED SKILLS			
Shows good listening skills			
Keeps attention on task at hand			
Can follow directions			
Works well in a group setting			
Works independently			

Comments _____

_____

_____

_____   _____
Resource Teacher   Classroom Teacher

FIGURE 7-4

PROGRESS REPORT — RESOURCE SPECIAL PROGRAMS

Grades 2-6

Name _____

Date of Birth _____

Age _____

Vision _____

Hearing _____

School _____ Grade _____

Date _____ Teacher _____

Resource Teacher _____

Setting: Individual (   ), Small Group (   ), Classroom (   )

Assessed by Speech Pathologist _____

Key
1. is working on
2. improvement shown
3. has completed
4. could benefit from extra help at home
5. little improvement, reassessment required

GROSS MOTOR SKILLS	December	March	June
Balance			
Walking			
Skipping			
Jumping — one foot			
— both feet			
Rhythm			
Catching a ball			
Throwing a ball			

Comments _____

_____

_____

	December	March	June
Bouncing a ball			
Muscular Strength			
General clumsiness or awkwardness			

Comments _____

_____

_____

LANGUAGE SKILLS

	December	March	June
Slow language development			
Ability to verbalize			
Ability to answer in sentence form			

Comments on weak areas: _____

_____

_____

PERCEPTION AND CONCEPT FORMATION

Ability to discriminate size			
Ability to discriminate right-left, up-down			
Tactile discrimination			
Spatial orientation			
Figure ground			
Perceptual motor			
Visual motor			
Time orientation			

	December	March	June
Body image			
Reverals in reading and in writing letters and numbers			
Ocular pursuit			
Fine motor coordination			
Visual memory			
Auditory memory			

Comments _____

_____

_____

THINKING PROCESSES

Ability for abstract reasoning			
Ability to form concepts			
Organization of thoughts			
Short-term memory — visual			
— auditory			
Long-term memory — visual			
— auditory			

Comments _____

_____

_____

ACADEMIC ACHIEVEMENT

READING

	December	March	June
— say alphabet			
— read alphabet			
— write alphabet			
— word attack skills			
— sight vocabulary			
— comprehension			
— drawing conclusions			
— sequencing			

Comments _____

_____

_____

MATH

	December	March	June
— say numerals			
— read numerals			
— write numerals			
— addition facts			
— subtraction facts			
— multiplication facts			
— division facts			
— simple problem solving			
— complex problem solving			

Comments _____

_____

_____

	December	March	June
Spelling			
Printing or writing			
Ability to organize work			
Ability to finish work			
Following direction — written			
— verbal			
Performance from day to day			

Comments _____

_____

_____

SOCIAL AND EMOTIONAL CHARACTERISTICS
(Check categories which apply to child)

Impulsive			
Explosive			
Emotional and impulse control			
Low tolerance for frustration			
Social competence frequently below average for age and measured intelligence			
Behavior often inappropriate for situation			
Possibly negative and aggressive to authority			
Antisocial behavior			
Shy and withdrawn			
Relationship with peer groups poor			

184

	December	March	June
Poor judgment in social and inter-personal situations			
Socially bold and aggressive			
Easy acceptance of others			
Takes part in class discussions			

Comments _____

_____

_____

ATTENTION AND CONCENTRATION

	December	March	June
Short attention span for age			
Overly distractible for age			
Impaired concentration ability			
Motor or verbal perseveration			
Inability to make decisions			
Gives up easily			
Easily upset			

Comments _____

_____

_____

MATERIALS TRIED AND COMMENTS:

_____

_____

_____

_____

_____   _____
Resource Teacher   Classroom Teacher

FIGURE 7-5

appropriate evaluation of special students in the regular classrooms can be done by establishing individualized goals and objectives. The student must be made aware of the specific tasks required to successfully earn a grade in the class.

As long as parents are aware of the fact that their child is on a special program, the regular school grading system can be used. School records must also show that the grades earned by the student are based on a modified program.

Anecdotal reports can be valuable in keeping parents informed about their child's progress.

Regardless of the method of reporting, the important points are as follows:

- The student must be challenged.
- Failure or success should not be predetermined.
- Grades should be determined by the student accomplishing realistic tasks.
- Performance in an academic setting is important for self-esteem and peer acceptance.
- Involvement in group projects is an excellent way of evaluating effort and contribution to the class.

The special class teacher can be a valuable resource in the evaluation of special students "mainstreamed" into regular classes. For example, assistance can be provided when establishing appropriate goals and performance objectives, selection of curriculum materials and teaching aids, organizing peer tutors, and grading of students.

EVALUATION IN SPECIAL CLASSES

Evaluation of students in special class programs should be done in terms of their progress toward meeting the goals and objectives previously listed in Chapter 6 which are appropriate for their age category.

Figures 7-6 and 7-7 are examples of forms used for high needs classes dealing with students, ages 9 to 13, based on the goals and objectives appropriate for this age category. The first form is composed of reading and language art skills, math skills evaluation, and life skills evaluation. This is followed by a similar student evaluation form designed for use with highest needs students ages 18-21. This form is a systematic way of reporting student progress toward meeting stated goals and objectives.

ANECDOTAL REPORTS

Another method of reporting student progress to parents is the use of anecdotal reports. (See Figure 7-8.) These may be used in conjunction with the aforegoing sample reports or independently.

PROGRESS REPORT — HIGH NEEDS STUDENTS

Name _____

Reporting Period _____

Times per cycle _____

Reading Evaluation Scale
1. does not perform task
2. often needs assistance
3. seldom needs assistance
4. has mastered skill

Acquisition of Reading Skills

   Reading Program

Analysis of Sounds in Words

Left to right eye movements		
Recognizes rhyming words		
Recognizes consonant sounds		
Associates consonant sounds with letters		
Knows long and short vowel sounds		
Recognizes consonant blends (st, fr, pr, etc.)		
and vowel combinations (ow, oa, oo, etc.)		
Analysis of Word Structure		
Recognizes basic sight words		
Recognizes root words		
Forms plurals by adding s, es, ies		
Recognizes compound words		
Adds common suffixes to root words		
Recognizes contractions		
Recognizes possessives		
Divides words into syllables		

Comprehension Skills

Picks out the main idea		
Finds details and facts in a story		
Understands literal meaning of word sentences, selections		
Follows instructions		
Sees relationships and makes comparisons		
Predicts outcomes and solutions		
Notes sequence of events		

Writing Skills

Copies sentences correctly		
Prints, writes legibly		
Writes original stories		
Uses periods, question marks, commas		
Uses capital letters		
Writes short friendly letters		
Keeps to main idea in stories		
Takes short dictation		

Spelling Skills

Developing spelling skills _____

Program _____

Lessons _____

Accuracy Level ___

Acquisition of Mathematics Skills

A. Numeration

Place Value

Reads numbers (6 digits)		
Knows place value (6 digits)		
Regroups three-digit numbers		

B. Computation

Addition

Adds, with sums to 18		
Adds, numbers in columns		
Adds, with carrying		

Subtraction

Subtracts with addends to 9		
Subtracts two-digit numbers		
Subtracts with regrouping		

Multiplication

Counts by numbers		
Computes multiplication facts		

Multiplies by 10, 100, 1000		
Multiplies digit by digit number		
Division		
Knows simple division facts		
Divides digit by digit number		
Divides with remainders		
Fractions		
Understands concept of fractions		
Beginning manipulation of fractions		
C. Applications		
Tells time		
Counts money		
Applies math to story problems		

Evaluation Scale

1. does not perform task
2. often needs assistance
3. seldom needs assistance
4. independently performs task

Acquisition of Life Skills

Cooperation and Community Life

This unit attempted to develop self-awareness and understanding of others, improve everyone's ability to communicate with others, introduced decision making techniques and encouraged development of the students' sense of "group."

190

Family Life

This unit focused on family structure, sex roles, work in the homes, communication in a family, and family origins. The purpose was to have students become aware of the role families play in communities and to become more tolerant of different family structures and changing sex roles (work).

The activities involved the following skills:

concentrating	
decision making	
discussing values	
drawing	
interviewing	
keeping a diary	
listening	
expressing feelings	
making collages	
ranking	
reading	
role playing	
sharing	
trusting	
writing	
voting	
greeting	
mapping community	
tabulating	

Comments:

_____

_____

_____

_____

Homeroom Teacher _____ _____
                                          Special Education Teacher

Parent's Signature _____

FIGURE 7-6

PROGRESS REPORT

Highest Needs Students, Ages 18-21

Evaluation Scale
1. does not perform task
2. often needs assistance
3. seldom needs assistance
4. has mastered skill

STUDENT'S NAME: _____

DATE: _____

INSTRUCTOR: _____

SUBJECT AREA: ACADEMIC

GOALS AND OBJECTIVES	CRITERIA MET	CRITERIA NOT MET	NOT APPLICABLE TO STUDENT	COMMENTS
1. To do activities to reinforce present academic skills				
2. To relate academic skills to general life skills and occupational skills				

Additional Comments:

SUBJECT AREA: RECREATIONAL

GOALS AND OBJECTIVES	CRITERIA MET	CRITERIA NOT MET	NOT APPLICABLE TO STUDENT	COMMENTS
1. Choosing their own leisure time activities				
2. Exposure to a variety of leisure time activities				
3. Stress the value of physical fitness				

SUBJECT AREA: RECREATIONAL

GOALS AND OBJECTIVES	CRITERIA MET	CRITERIA NOT MET	NOT APPLICABLE TO STUDENT	COMMENTS
4. Learning about the recreational and leisure time facilities in their own community and how to access them				

Additional Comments:

SUBJECT AREA: PREVOCATIONAL

GOALS AND OBJECTIVES	CRITERIA MET	CRITERIA NOT MET	NOT APPLICABLE TO STUDENT	COMMENTS
1. To demonstrate an understanding of skills necessary for work experience by completion of specific objectives: a. money management and banking				
b. communication skills				
c. use of telephone				
d. kitchen management				
e. time management				
f. following established work routines				
g. filling out applications				

SUBJECT AREA: PREVOCATIONAL

GOALS AND OBJECTIVES	CRITERIA MET	CRITERIA NOT MET	NOT APPLICABLE TO STUDENT	COMMENTS
h. proper dress and behavior during interviews				
i. utilizing transportation systems				
j. doing laundry, housecleaning, house maintenance, outdoor yard work				

Additional Comments:

SUBJECT AREA: VOCATIONAL

GOALS AND OBJECTIVES	CRITERIA MET	CRITERIA NOT MET	NOT APPLICABLE TO STUDENT	COMMENTS
1. Full time employment either competitive or sheltered (at the end of their program)				
2. To master the steps necessary to apply for and retain a job				
3. Understand and appreciate the value and dignity of work				
4. To understand their own employment strengths and weaknesses				

SUBJECT AREA: VOCATIONAL

GOALS AND OBJECTIVES	CRITERIA MET	CRITERIA NOT MET	NOT APPLICABLE TO STUDENT	COMMENTS
5. To develop an understanding of how the employment system operates				
6. To demonstrate all of the above through successful work experience				

Additional Comments:

SUBJECT AREA: SOCIAL AND EMOTIONAL

GOALS AND OBJECTIVES	CRITERIA MET	CRITERIA NOT MET	NOT APPLICABLE TO STUDENT	COMMENTS
1. To develop socially acceptable adult behavior				
2. To understand and successfully deal with their own emotions				
3. To understand and assert their individual rights				
4. To understand and appropriately deal with their own sexuality				
5. To understand, accept, and like themselves and others				

Additional Comments:

SUBJECT AREA: LIFE SKILLS

GOALS AND OBJECTIVES	CRITERIA MET	CRITERIA NOT MET	NOT APPLICABLE TO STUDENT	COMMENTS
1. To learn to live as independently as possible (group home or super-vised apartment)				
2. To develop self-sufficient personal hygiene				
3. To understand good nutrition principles				
4. To develop pro-per communica-tion skills				
5. To develop prob-lem solving tech-niques				
6. To develop good health, safety, first aid skills				
7. To develop a good sense of values				
8. To learn about and utilize com-munity resources				
9. To understand personal learning strengths and weaknesses				

Additional Comments:

196

SUBJECT AREA: INTEGRATION ACTIVITIES WITH ADULTS IN THE COMMUNITY

GOALS AND OBJECTIVES	CRITERIA MET	CRITERIA NOT MET	NOT APPLICABLE TO STUDENT	COMMENTS
1. FRIDAY LUNCHEON a. shop				
b. prepare and plan menu				
c. set table				
d. serve dinner				
e. chef				
f. appropriate social skills				
2. NOTEPAPER a. makes notepaper independently				
b. sales				
c. money awareness (able to make change)				
3. INTERACTION WITH VOLUNTEERS a. establishes friendship with age-appropriate volunteers				
b. establishes relationship with community resource person				
4. CHRISTMAS TEA AND CRAFT SALE a. participates in making crafts independently				

197

SUBJECT AREA:	INTEGRATION ACTIVITIES WITH ADULTS IN THE COMMUNITY			
GOALS AND OBJECTIVES	CRITERIA MET	CRITERIA NOT MET	NOT APPLICABLE TO STUDENT	COMMENTS
b. participates in preparing baked goods				
c. money aware-ness (able to make change)				
d. sales				
e. organizational ability				
5. Improved positive self-esteem and confidence through commun-ity-integration activities				

Additional Comments:

FIGURE 7-7

ANECDOTAL PROGRESS REPORT

School: _____

Name: _____ Term: 1   2   3

Class: _____ Date: _____

Teacher: _____

_____

_____

_____

_____

_____

_____

_____

_____

_____

_____

_____

_____

_____

Teacher's Signature

FIGURE 7-8

199

The advantages of using anecdotal reports are:

- They describe, in everyday language, to parents concrete examples of their child's progress.

- They provide an opportunity to describe the child's learning strengths as well as areas of need.

- They afford teachers an opportunity to personalize student records. This is especially important in a system that uses numerical or letter grades to report predetermined curriculum standards.

- They make it possible to isolate, in time, specific gains made by an individual child.

Although we may never reach the perfection alluded to by Martin Buber in his quote at the beginning of this chapter, we must continually strive for this perfection if we are to offer the best possible services to students and their parents through our school systems.

Bibliography

Adams, Norma, "Integrated Ideas for Language Arts," unpublished, Dartmouth District School Board, c/o Physical Education Dept., 95 Victoria Road, Dartmouth, NS, B3A 1V2.

Agard, Judith; McCullough, Nancy; and Santangelo-Broderson, Lynda, *Marathon: A Program for Teaching Social Behaviors Needed for Work and Community Living*, Stanfield Film Associates, Santa Monica, CA, 1983.

Ainsworth, Barbara; Trautman, David; and Layton, James, *Reading Labels and Signs*, Hampden Publications, Baltimore, MD, 1979.

Allmond, Phyllis, and Moch, Valerie, *Pacemaker Arithmetic Program*, Fearon-Pitman Publishers, Inc., Belmont, CA, 1974.

Anastasi, A., *Psychological Testing*, 4th ed., Macmillan Publishing Company, New York, 1976.

Anderson, Donald, G., *New Practice Readers*, McGraw-Hill Book Co., New York, 1978.

Anderson, Val, and Smart, David, *Primary Learning Skills Program*, Benefic Press, Chicago, IL, 1980.

Baratta-Lorton, Mary, *Mathematics Their Way*, Addison-Wesley Publishing Co., Reading, MA, 1976.

Barnes, Cheryle, "Helpful Hints for Parents: Readiness for School Begins at Home," unpublished.

Barnes, Cheryle, and Parush, Barbara, "Everything You Wanted to Know About Preschool Screening, but Were Afraid to Ask," unpublished.

Barnes, David B., *The Bigger They Are, the Harder*, Submission to Federal Government Task Force, October, 1984.

Beswick, Joan (ed.), *The Hearing Impaired Child In Public School: A Guide for Administrators and Teachers*, Atlantic Provinces Resource Center for the Hearing Handicapped, Amherst, Nova Scotia, 1985.

Blackhurst, A. Edward, and Berdine, William, H., *An Introduction to Special Education*, Little, Brown and Co., Boston, MA, 1981.

Blau, Melinda, *Following Written Directions, Canadian Reading Skills Series*, Edu-Media, Kitchener, Ontario, 1979.

Blum, Gloria, and Blum, Barry, *Feeling Good About Yourself*, Feeling Good Associates, Mill Valley, CA, 1981.

Bluma, Sjetal, *Portage Guide to Early Education*, Portage, WI, 1976.

Buros, Oscar (ed.), *The Eighth Mental Measurements Yearbook*, Gryphon Press, Highland Park, NJ, 1978.

Burt and Brower, *Education for Sexuality: Concepts and Programs for Teaching*, W.B. Saunders Co., Philadelphia, PA, 1970.

Bush, W.J., and Giles, M.T., *Aids to Psycholinguistic Teaching*, Charles E. Merrill, Co., Columbus, OH, 1969.

C.A.C.L.D., "The Parent As Advocate," C.A.C.L.D., Ottawa, Ontario, 1981.

Campbell, Wendy, *Aqua Percept*, Pointe-Claire, Quebec, 1976.

Canfield, Jack, and Wells, Harold C., *100 Ways to Enhance Self-Concept in the Classroom*, Prentice-Hall, Inc., Englewood Cliffs, NJ, 1976.

Cantwell, D.P., *The Hyperactive Child*, Spectrum Publications, Inc., New York, 1975.

Carlaw, R., and Raithby, P., *Applying Mathematics*, McGraw-Hill Book Co., New York, 1967.

Connors, C.K., *Food Additives and Hyperactive Children*, Plenum Press, New York, 1981.

Dade County Public Schools, *Turn About — It's Your Turn to Teach*, Dade County Public Schools, Miami, FL, 1975.

Deiner, Penny Lou, *Resources for Teaching Young Children with Special Needs*, Harcourt Brace Jovanovich, San Diego, CA.

Dinkmeyer, D., and Dinkmeyer D. Jr., *Developing Understanding of Self and Others*, American Guidance Services, Circle Pines, MN, 1972.

Donlon, Edward, and Burton, Louise, *The Severely and Profoundly Handicapped: A Practical Approach to Teaching*, Grune & Stratton, New York, 1976.

Dubnoff, Belle; Chambers, Irene; and Schaefer, John, *Dubnoff School Program Series*, Teaching Systems and Resources Inc., Hingham, MA, 1968.

Dupont, Henry; Gardner, O.S.; and Brody, David, *Toward Affective Development*, American Guidance Services, Circle Pines, MN, 1984.

Elrich, Thomas F., *Forms in Your Life*, Modern Curriculum Press, Cleveland, OH, 1981.

Farrow, Elvira, and Hill, Carol, *Montessori on a Limited Budget*, Montessori Workshop, Ithaca, NY, 1975.

Feingold, Benjamin, *Why Your Child Is Hyperactive*, Random House, New York, 1974.

Feingold, Helene, and Feingold, Benjamin, *The Feingold Cookbook for Hyperactive Children and Others with Problems Associated with Food Additives and Salicylates*, Random House, New York, 1979.

Fernald, G., *Remedial Techniques in Basic Subjects*, McGraw-Hill Book Co., New York, 1943.

Frost, Jack, and Ratliff, Linda, *Workers We Know*, Chronicle Guidance Publications Inc., Moravia, NY, 1973.

Frostig, Marianne, *Frostig Visual Perception Program*, Follett Publishing Co., Chicago, IL, 1973.

Gallogley, Gloria, et.al., *Growing Up*, Novalis Publishing Co., Ottawa, Ontario, 1984.

Gagné, Robert, *Skill Modes in Mathematics*, Science Research Associates, Chicago, IL, 1974.

Glasser, William, *Schools Without Failure*, Harper & Row, New York, 1975.

Glasser, William, *Reality Therapy: A New Approach to Psychiatry*, Harper & Row, New York, 1975.

Glassman, Martyn, and Kisiow, Elaine, *Cooperation and Community Life*, Cooperation College of Canada, Saskatoon, Saskatchewan, 1983.

Glatthorn, Allan, and Christensen, Jane, *Patterns of Communicating*, D.C. Heath & Co., Lexington, MA, 1973.

Goldbert, H.R., and Greenberger, Bernard, *The Job Ahead: A Career Reading Series*, *(4)*, Science Research Associates, Chicago, 1977.

Goodman, Kenneth, and Goodman, Yetta, *Linguistics, Psycholinguistics and the Teaching of Reading*, International Reading Association, Newark, DE, 1980.

Gordon, Sol, *The Teenage Survival Book*, Harper & Row, Scranton, PA, 1981.

Gordon, Sol, and Everly, Kathleen, "Increasing Self-Esteem in Vulnerable Students,"

Impact '85, Vol. 9, pages 1-4, Ed-U Press, Fayetteville, NY, 1985.

Gossage, Loyce, and Briggs, Milton, *Mathematics Skill Builder*, South-Western Publishing Co., Cincinnati, OH, 1969.

Gray, Davon, "Home Based Early Intervention: The Story of Susan," *Teaching Exceptional Children*, Vol. 12, pages 79-81, Reston, VA, 1980.

Greenberg, Mal (ed.), *Basic Skills Program Reading*, King Features, LSR Learning Associates, Inc., Old Bethpage, NY, 1977.

Hannah, Marta; Millhouse, John; Sauvageot, Audrey; Froelick, Arlene; Zidar, Phyllis; Spinks, Nancy; and Landau, Paula, *SCIL: Systematic Curriculum for Independent Living*, Academic Therapy Publications, San Rafael, CA, 1977.

Hayden, Margaret, et.al., *Mathematics for Daily Use*, Doubleday, New York, 1980.

Hehner, Barbara (ed.), *Blissymbolics for Use*, Blissymbolics Communication Institute, Toronto, Ontario, 1980.

Hill, Sylvia (ed.), *SRA Schoolhouse Comprehension Patterns*, Science Research Associates, Chicago, 1974.

Johnson, D., and Mylkebust, H.R., *Learning Disabilities: Educational Principles and Practices*, Grune & Stratton, New York, 1967.

Kaufman, Alan, S., *Intelligent Testing with the WISC-R*, John Wiley & Sons, New York, 1979.

Kaufman, Alan, and Kaufman, Nadeen; *Kaufman Assessment Battery for Children*, American Guidance Services, Inc., Circle Pines, MN, 1983.

Kaufman, Alan; Kaufman, Nadeen; and Goldsmith, Bonnie, *Kaufman Sequential or Simultaneous*, American Guidance Services, Inc., Circle Pines, MN, 1984.

Kinsbourne, M., and Caplan, P.J., *Childrens Learning and Attention Problems*, Little, Brown & Co., Boston, MA, 1979.

Laubach, Frank C., and Kirk, Elizabeth M., *Laubach Reading Program*, New Readers Press, Syracuse, NY, 1968.

Laubach, Frank C., and Kirk, Elizabeth M., *Laubach Way to Reading*, Laubach Literacy, Syracuse, NY, 1981.

Levin, Beatrice J., *Real Life Reading: A Scholastic Program in Functional Reading*, Scholastic Book Services, Lyndhurst, NJ.

Lichtenstein, Robert, and Ireton, Harry, *Preschool Screening: Identifying Young Children with Developmental and Educational Problems*, Grune & Stratton Inc., Orlando, FL, 1984.

Liddle, Wm. (ed.), *Reading for Concepts*, McGraw-Hill Book Co., New York, 1977.

Lieberman, Laurence M., *Preventing Special Education: For Those Who Don't Need It,"* GloWorm Publications, Newton, MA, 1984.

Linkenhoker, Dan, and McCarron, Lawrence, *Street Survival Skills Questionnaire*, Common Market Press, Dallas, TX, 1983.

MacMillan, D.L., *Behavior Modification in Education*, Macmillan Publishing Co., New York, 1973.

MacNeil, Francis X., "Daniel: An Education Success Story," *Journal of Education*, Nova Scotia Department of Education, Halifax, Nova Scotia, 1981.

Manolakes, George, et.al., *Try, Experiences for Young Children*, Noble & Noble Publishers, Inc., New York, 1967.

Manolson, Ayala, *It Takes Two to Talk: A Hanen Early Language Parent Guide Book*, Hanen Early Language Resource Centre, Toronto, 1983.

Martin, William, *Instant Readers*, Holt, Reinhart & Winston, New York, 1970.

May, Rollo, *Power and Innocence: A Search for Sources of Violence*, Norton, New York, 1972.

McDiarmid; Peterson; and Sutherland, *Loving and Learning: Interactions with Your Child from Birth to Three*, Harcourt Brace Jovanovich, San Diego, CA, 1975.

Merkley, Elaine, *Becoming a Learner*, Charles E. Merrill Co., Columbus, OH, 1972.

Moss, Barbara, *SAIL: Skills to Achieve Independent Living*, Melton Peninsula Inc., Dallas, TX, 1979.

Nelson, Leslie, and Lorbeer, George, *Science Activities for Elementary Children*, Wm. C. Brown & Co., Dubuque, IA, 1976.

Nelson, L.D., and Liedtke, W., *Mathematical Experiences in Early Childhood*, Encyclopedia Britannica Publications, Chicago, IL, 1982.

Novakovich, H.; Smith, J.; and Tecgardey C., *Target on Language*, Christ Church Child Center, Bethesda, MD, 1973.

O'Brien, Mary Consilia, Sr., *The Non-Coping Child*, Academic Therapy Publications, Novato, CA, 1978.

Quinn, Treva, *Mafex Math Survivial Series*, Mafex Associates, Johnstown, PA, 1980.

Raths, Louis; Wasserman, Selma; and Wasserman, Jack, *Thinking Skills Development Program*, Benefic Press, Chicago, IL, 1982.

Richardson, Hazel A., *Games for Junior and Senior High Schools*, Burgess Publishing Co., Minneapolis, MN, 1957.

Rogers, Carl, *Freedom to Learn: A View of What Education Might Become*, Charles E. Merrill, Columbus, OH, 1969.

Ross, D.M., and Ross, S.A., *Hyperactivity — Research, Theory, Action*, John Wiley & Sons, New York, 1976.

Rutledge, Earl, "Application of Audiotutorial Teaching Utilizing Rate Controlled Speech Technologies," unpublished, 1983.

Sanford, Adrian, et.al., *Audio Reading Kit*, Educational Progress, Tulsa, OK, 1976.

Schirmer, Gene, *Performance Objectives for Preschool Children*, Delta-Schoolcraft Intermediate School District, Gladstone, MI, 1974.

Simpson, D.D., and Nelson, A.E., "Breathing Control and Attention Training," U.S. Educational Resources Information Centre, *ERIC Document*, ED063723, 1977.

Sullivan, M.D., and Howlett, James S., *Programmed Math*, McGraw-Hill Book Co., New York, 1975.

Sullivan, M.D., *Programmed Reading Series*, Webster Division, McGraw-Hill Book Co., New York, 1973.

Swanson, H.L., and Watson, B.L., *Educational and Psychological Assessment of Exceptional Children: Theories, Strategies and Applications*, C.V. Mosby Co., St. Louis, MO, 1982.

Taylor, Edward, and Hamilton, Garry, *On the Job: Now Is Tomorrow Series*, The Book Society of Canada, Ltd., Agincourt, Ontario, Canada, 1979.

Taylor, Ellen, and Stewart, Charles, *Practicing Occupational Reading Skills*, Random House, New York, 1982.

Thorndike, R.L., and Hagen, E., *Measurement and Evaluation in Psychology and Education*, 4th ed., John Wiley & Sons, New York, 1977.

Turner, Richard H., *Turner Career Guidance Series*, Follett Publishing Co., Chicago, IL, 1974.

Ungerleider, Dorothy Fink, *Reading, Writing and Rage*, Jalmar Press, Rolling Hill Estates, CA, 1985.

Valett, Robert E., *The Remediation of Learning Disabilities: A Handbook of Psychoeducational Resource Programs*, Fearon, Belmont, CA, 1967.

Walling, Jean; Baugh, Carol; Moss, Barbara; and Ort, Elizabeth (ed.), *Radea: Testing and Remediation*, Melton Peninsula Inc., Dallas, TX, 1976.

White, Burton, "The Critical Importance of Hearing Ability," *The Center for Parent Education Newsletter*, Vol. 1; Nos. 3 and 4, Newton, MA, 1979.

White, Burton, *The First Three Years of Life*, Prentice-Hall, Inc., Englewood Cliffs, NJ, 1975.

Whitworth, John, and Sutton, Dorothy, *WISC-R Compilation: What to Do Now That You Know the Score*, Academic Therapy Publications, Novato, CA, 1978.

Wittels, Harriet, and Greisman, John, *How to Spell It: A Dictionary of Commonly Misspelled Words*, (originally published as *The Perfect Speller*), Grosset & Dunlap, New York, 1973.

Wood, Bob, *Environmental Science*, Holt, Rinehart & Winston of Canada Ltd., Toronto, 1975.

Wood, John D., *Using Money Series*, Frank E. Richard Publishing Co., Liverpool, NY, 1982.

Woodruff, G.W.; Moore, G.N.; and Nadig, N.S., *Spelling Words in Use*, Curriculum Associates, North Billerica, MA, 1974.

Ysseldyke, James E., and Salvia, John, *Assessment in Special and Remedial Education* (2nd ed.), Houghton Mifflin Co., Boston, MA, 1981.

Index